Towards a Digital Renaissance

For Janet,

Lots of love

Jrey

Towards a Digital Renaissance

The evolution of
creativity, values and
business from cyberspace
to the metaverse

Jeremy Silver

PROFILE
EDITIONS

First published in Great Britain in 2022 by
Profile Editions, an imprint of Profile Books
29 Cloth Fair
London
EC1A 7JQ
www.profileeditions.com

Copyright © Jeremy Silver, 2022

1 3 5 7 9 10 8 6 4 2

Typeset in Sabon by MacGuru Ltd
Printed and bound in Great Britain by
Clays Ltd, Elcograf S.p.A.

A CIP catalogue record for this book is available from the British Library.

ISBN 978 1 80081 717 3
eISBN 978 1 80081 515 5

Contents

INTRODUCTION

{'For What It's Worth', Buffalo Springfield, 1966}

This is a book about digital disruption at an industrial scale – how the music industry took the hit first, twenty years ago, and how it felt to be in the middle of that tsunami and being rolled around by it.

It's also about digital disruption from the disrupters' perspective: four companies that thought they would be sprinters but discovered they needed to be marathon runners and how, in these different cases, the relationships between entrepreneur and investor changed.

And finally, we explore digital disruption from a national perspective. How national policy-based interventions work, what the landscape of innovation looks like, what works well and where it has shortcomings.

We explore the Digital Catapult – a unique institution that feels a little like the MIT Media Lab of the 1990s, using public funds to address the challenges and opportunities of digital disruption from a policy perspective, an industrial sector viewpoint and from the entrepreneurial position.

Throughout these discussions, we shall also explore the shifting climate of business culture and values. We'll look at what the expectations of corporate culture should be and what a good, tech-driven business actually is.

Finally, we will head into a meditation on the metaverse and consider how all these factors may work themselves out in Web 3.0 and what might be needed to avoid a future metaverse dystopia.

This is also a personal book, about what life is like being an innovator inside a corporate world and about how to take the courage of your convictions and escape the corporate world into the wilder and looser environs of entrepreneurialism.

Trying to innovate is hard. I was the media director at Virgin Records in 1993. I was supposed to be publicising bands, not staying up late figuring out how to access university libraries in the United States over the internet.

I was so determined to try to share the importance of what I was playing with and how I knew it was going to change the industry, but it was hard to get anyone's attention. They were all focused on business as usual. I once chased Rupert Perry, the President of EMI Europe, along a corridor and into the washroom in an attempt to get him to pay attention to our new young internet programme. That was in 1997. The following year, I was transferred to Los Angeles to be the EMI gatekeeper for internet deals. I left a year later to move up to San Francisco and found a start-up myself.

Then it turned out that being an innovator in a start-up is hard too, especially when the markets collapse around you and a worldwide terrorist event happens (the attacks on 11 September 2001: 9/11).

The truth is that I have had imposter syndrome throughout my entire career. I never was entirely sure that I knew what I was doing. The narrative is powerful because it gives you the story you can tell yourself. If you can't believe your own story nobody else will either.

Everyone needs a narrative – governments, industries,

start-ups – even investors. And of course narratives clash – creators and label execs clashed. Labels got angry because the Featured Artists Coalition was undermining the narrative. The story that the content industries had decided to tell government was at odds with the story the artists were telling. Ministers need at least to appear to listen.

And in the investor corner, the narrative that says unicorns are best remains troubling and has had disastrous consequences; it ruined people's lives. The investors' argument that we need more unicorns was a sophisticated acknowledgement that they wanted to turn a fictional creature into a reality and that money had the power to do that. But more often than not, they have proved that unicorns are indeed a fiction.

More about imposter syndrome. I always felt like an outsider. When I was at a label I could never discuss football – I knew nothing about it then and I know nothing about it now. My son tells me I support Arsenal. When I was in Silicon Valley, it was clear that the Valley is a club and Sand Hill Road is the clubhouse. I didn't feel like I was a member – I was not a techie with a computer science degree – I was a music industry guy trying to work out whether the Valley was cool or not. I was probably overly concerned that Uplister would not be seen as cool and therefore would not appeal to the labels. Truth was, Uplister disrupted the labels' narrative so they were never going to help us.

So what is the profile of a true innovator? We spend some time in this book trying to figure that out. It certainly includes a high degree of creative destruction. Every institution, every company I worked in, disappeared after I went there. My university – Cardiff – became part of the University of Wales. Bedford College in London was merged with Royal Holloway – lost its lovely Regent's Park campus and moved to Egham.

Virgin-EMI no longer exist as independent companies but are a part of Universal Music Group, Uplister folded, Sibelius went to Avid. Semetric went to Apple. Shazam went to Apple. Each of them was taken apart and put back together again differently, acquired, consolidated – disappeared. None of the jobs that I did in my entire career until I got to Digital Catapult had existed before I joined or had been done by anyone else.

What an amazing amount of change. Like a vast game of *Minecraft*.

*

This book begins, in the last days of the analogue music industry, with vinyl records giving way to aluminium CDs and digital files looming on the horizon. It closes with what might be the end – or at least the end of the beginning – of the digital revolution that over the past three decades has swept away almost all trace of that analogue world.

But what will come next? We stand at the dawn of a new revolution – one that promises to erode the distinction between the online and offline worlds. The emergence of the so-called metaverse promises an incredible range of new possibilities for the ways we live and work – and also new perils to avoid and overcome. How can we chart a course through this exciting but risky world?

In some ways, we've been here before. Back in the early 1990s, the internet was an anarchic realm visited by only a few intrepid souls and understood by even fewer – even though it would revolutionise the way music was made, distributed and sold in little more than a decade. At the onset of this period of immense change, I was working at the heart of the recording industry, then at the height of its glamour, wealth and pomp. Intoxicating though it could be, I found the internet more intoxicating still, with its promise of limitless connectivity and freedom.

That promise was fulfilled by the emergence in 1993 of two novel technologies – mp3 and the world wide web – that conspired to create an existential threat to the global recording industry, in the form of a tsunami of file-sharing. The major companies initially tried to ignore file-sharing, then to sue it out of existence – targeting not just the creators of sharing software, but its own potential customers. By the time they accepted it might be better to go with the flow, it was too late. For all their might, they failed to turn the tide for many years.

Eager to make the future rather than be drowned by it, I moved on to an entrepreneur's life – amid the anything-goes dotcom mania of Silicon Valley and the turbulence of companies crossing the divide from the old, analogue world of discs and boxes to the new, online universe of files and software. Over the next decade, I enjoyed some spectacular successes and suffered some highly instructive failures running and selling two businesses and sitting on the boards of several more. I suspect we learn far more from our failures than our successes, but we'll come back to that. I looked on as more and more industries followed music into the digital realm, and had a hand in helping a few along the way. I had a front-row seat for the dotcom boom, the rise of digital titans like Apple, Google and Facebook and now for the emergence of the metaverse.

When I sat down to write this book, I intended to recount that journey, and to relate what I see as the opportunities we collectively discovered (and sometimes squandered) and the challenges we faced (and sometimes failed) along the way, tracking the evolution of the internet and of digital society around us along the way. As I progressed, however, I realised there were many questions we still haven't answered satisfactorily today.

How do people and companies respond to rapid technological evolution and profound change? Where do founders get the tenacity and self-belief needed to continue their missions against all odds? What is the essence of 'good' entrepreneurship and investment?

The answers to these questions, in the first thirty years of the digital revolution, have not had results we would regard as wholly admirable. People and companies react to change by embracing either denial or disruption, neither of which are entirely productive responses. Founders have been motivated by unimaginable levels of wealth and power, untrammelled by considerations of ethics or justice. And 'good' business has come to mean aggressive, amoral growth at all costs, regardless of the price that ends up being paid by creators, customers or society.

Despite all the positives that digital technology has brought us, we have experienced a staggering change of perspective, with a dawning realisation that the hero brands of the dotcom boom – Facebook, Google, Amazon, Apple – have become today's villainous digital monopolists. Responsible, passionate entrepreneurs building stable businesses have often been elbowed aside by edgier operators promising overnight fortunes, while both creators and customers were ruthlessly exploited. Wrapped inside that is the realisation that the alpha-male, scale-at-all-costs aggression championed by Silicon Valley, and exemplified by its greatest unicorns, has led to toxic work environments, economic and social inequities, and socially harmful outcomes.

As I described in *Digital Medieval*, the 2013 precursor to this book, the original internet dream of freedom and sharing has given way to a new medievalism – with the once-freewheeling digital realm divided into enclaves ruthlessly controlled by a handful of imperial tech demigods, under whom countless cyber serfs toil for meagre reward. Technologies that appear to bring us together have instead all too often driven us apart. The more our lives have tilted towards digital interaction, the more we've seen how it can take us to the brink of dehumanisation and extremism.

More recently, the Covid-19 pandemic led to a great lacuna in our lives and an acceleration of these trends. For those of us fortunate enough not to be gravely affected, it enforced a pause for thought – a cessation, for a while, of the everyday course of life, work and play. And that cessation of physical activity led to the rapid expansion of our digital existence. Every aspect of human life – talking to friends, holding business meetings, seeking professional advice – was conducted within the confines of windows on screens. In the space of months, we adopted technologies and ways of working that might have otherwise taken years to become the norm.

Companies like the one I have had the privilege to lead – Digital Catapult, the UK's authority on advanced digital technology – experienced great gains in efficiency and productivity as we locked ourselves to our screens and focused our conversations on what 'really mattered' and what 'really needed to get done'. Small wonder that we are trying to preserve some of those benefits within our new business-as-usual model of hybrid working. But at the same time, we have become even more aware of the fact that we can't afford to lose the richness of face-to-face, human-to-human interactions. Without the empathy and roundedness of relationships that such interactions bring, it is harder to build trust, stumble on serendipitous connections and dream up imaginative opportunities.

Lockdowns and the effective closing of society caused by the pandemic gave social media even more power and influence over our lives and particularly over the lives of adolescents, with negative consequences that we are still struggling to understand. But some of the results have been easy to see: a shifting of political discourse to the very edges of previous acceptability and a rise in groupthink and mob rule in many parts of society from cultural analysis to the US Capitol. Respect for hard facts and considered debate is in decline: the very basis of our precious Western democracy feels threatened.

The digital story is not over, though. There is still great power and great potential in emerging digital technologies. We have generated more data in the last two decades than in the entire previous history of civilisation. We are now starting to distil small amounts of knowledge and understanding out of this data. We are starting to enrich and empower our own lives and the lives of others by using the tools. And we are starting to mobilise for social change by using the connections. We are piecing together narratives and plans that are helping us to shape and navigate our continually evolving digital world. And in the face of a growing techlash, innovators have to remain curious, positive, optimistic and open to achieve our goals and however naïve it may seem, we must believe in utopian and not dystopian outcomes.

So we need to think hard about what we really want from the next suite of emerging technologies, which promise to be every bit as revolutionary in their own ways as the world wide web was in its day. As with the original medieval period, the continued march of technology holds out the promise of a new flowering of creativity and innovation: a digital renaissance, if you will. For all that the competitive landscape has changed dramatically over the past three decades, some things have remained constant: the pace of change, the addictiveness of connectivity and screens. But it's my fascination with innovation that still makes me want to get up in the morning and find out what the future holds. There are choices to be made, and those choices are more obviously ours to make today than ever before.

There were several good, simple reasons why music led the way when it came to digital technology. Music's appeal is global; even language barriers pose only a limited challenge to its appeal across borders. Its product was easily turned into very small digital files that could be easily shared across the early slow-moving internet. So music led the way in developing the commercial and social potential of the web more than any other field. Where music led, everything else followed: books, films, television and then shopping, travel, accommodation, dating and pretty much everything else.

I've brought the lessons I learned working in and around the music industry to bear in my role as the chief executive of Digital Catapult, and the first half of this book relates how those experiences – in cyberspace, in Silicon Valley and in the UK – have informed my views on the future of digital business. The job of the Catapult is to encourage the development and early adoption of emerging digital technologies in UK companies – whether in start-ups, scale-ups or traditional businesses. We operate primarily in the creative industries and the manufacturing sector. While the focus of this book is largely on the creative side of things, we often see the relevance of experiences in creative companies to how the impact of digitisation is felt in traditional heavy industrial companies.

The UK is one of the world's most advanced digital economies, but there is still plenty of distance to go, and still plenty of scope for the next generation of digital technologies – immersive environments, artificial intelligence, distributed ledgers – to be adopted more thoughtfully than the previous ones. Witnessing the evolution of technology and business models over the past thirty years has left me with a distinct sense of peril as we contemplate the next great leap forward in the digital revolution: the so-called metaverse. That term, 'the metaverse', is taken from one of the founding texts of cyberculture, Neal Stephenson's 1992 sci-fi novel *Snow Crash*, and represents the ultimate ascendance of the online world, to the point where it equals and even subsumes our corporeal existence. If *that's* what's in store, we had better make sure it's the kind of place we really want to live in. For many of us, it promises the ultimate freedom to be whoever you want to be: to go anywhere and do anything, almost indistinguishably from the 'real' thing. But if being locked down taught us anything, it is that there is no substitute for the 'real thing' of human interaction, face to face. The excitement offered by some visions of the metaverse is that it is as much an escape from real life as it is a substitute for it.

Unfortunately, there are worrying signs that the metaverse will be built by the same people, using the same methods, as the current online world – and that the resulting harms could be even greater. That would be an enormous missed opportunity – perhaps the *final* missed opportunity of the digital revolution. To avoid that, we need to look for alternative perspectives hidden in the backwaters of the great river of technological and business development that has roared along over three tumultuous decades. To answer my opening questions 'how do we create the conditions that will enable responsible technology-driven entrepreneurship and maintain sight of our values?' undoubtedly, we need to chart our course according to business values, not just financial returns, and tempered by social considerations, not just investors' priorities.

Those business values and social considerations are embedded in the work we do at Digital Catapult and, we hope, in the companies and organisations we help to embrace the possibilities of digital technology. It is by no means easy, but the effort is worthwhile because the prize is great. I hope that the metaverse, where so many strands of emergent technology are set to converge, can also be where many strands of a kinder, more inclusive, more diverse and more forgiving business environment converge – where relationships transcend transactions, where fair prices are paid for fairly created products, where openness trumps the proprietary, and where our virtual selves are true to our real selves. That would finally deliver on the original dream of the internet, and the metaverse: a digital renaissance.

1

INTO CYBERSPACE

{'Starman', David Bowie, *The Rise and Fall of Ziggy Stardust and the Spiders from Mars*, 1972}

I grew up in a house that was full of discs; it contained as big a record collection as any home reasonably could. My father was addicted to record shops, where he would scour the racks for bargains – often collecting multiple different recordings of a piece of music. His great love was classical music and particularly opera, for which, as it happens, I have yet to acquire a taste. Perhaps that was in part a reaction to living in a house full of it; perhaps it's just a matter of personal taste. Be that as it may, from a young age I became attuned to both the financial and cultural value of recorded music.

I was also interested in music-making, forever trying to learn to make pleasant sounds from instruments, including various forms of pipe and flute. At the age of twelve, I saved up enough (with my sister's help) to acquire a second-hand Grundig TK23 reel-to-reel tape recorder with which I recorded a variety of family events, with varying degrees of cooperation. I was also recording and experimenting with my own scratch-built instruments: biscuit tins surrounded by rubber bands with a microphone nestled inside. A more capable Revox later allowed me to experiment with editing, overdubbing and mixing: slowing down sounds of the dawn chorus to listen to birdsong at half speed, for example.

For all that, I never had any expectations of a career in music. My academic training was in English, which I studied up to PhD level. But when I started looking for a job, the advert that caught my attention was for a research officer position at the National Sound Archive (NSA), which sounded like a fun place to work – and so it was. When I started there, in the mid-1980s, it was in a Queen Anne townhouse that backed onto the Royal Albert Hall in Kensington, with massive basements filled with discs, tapes and wax cylinders, while boxes full of old shellac BBC transcription discs lurked in biscuit tins under the stairs. It was one of the largest record collections in the world. Even bigger than my dad's – although it too had begun life in cardboard boxes under the bed of its founder, Patrick Saul.

Walking through it as I arrived every morning, I was bombarded by sounds: the howling of Arctic wolves mingled with rare recordings of Dohnanyi violin concertos, while an early speech by Churchill crackled out from somewhere else. My first job was to create a directory of non-commercial recordings, which meant touring around the UK's museums and libraries to find out what collections they had. A lot of it was oral history, but some was more offbeat: the mechanical industrial sounds of knitting needles being manufactured in Sheffield, for example.

The NSA also provided my memorable first encounter with the music industry. As part of the British Library, it aimed to secure a copy of every commercial recording released in the UK. But whereas there is a legal requirement that publishers deposit a copy of every new book with the British Library, there is no such 'statutory deposit' requirement when it comes to audio recordings. As a result, NSA staff periodically had to visit the offices of the major record companies and persuade them to keep the Archive on their distribution list for promotional copies of new releases. Since this cost them money for no return other than the thanks of the nation, they did not always see why they should.

I joined one of the archivists on a visit to meet Maurice Oberstein, then chairman of PolyGram Records. He was a flamboyant New Yorker, well known in the industry for being perpetually accompanied by his dog, Eric, and for the strange vocal tic that turned his voice into a falsetto whenever he became exercised by something or someone.

'Obie' sat at his desk, at the far end of a long narrow office, its walls lined with shelves of CDs, which were then a novel format – and which had stopped arriving at the NSA. We explained our mission, noting that his company's CDs represented an unparalleled cultural treasure trove that would be invaluable to future researchers and posterity. We assured him that subsequent generations would be eternally grateful if he ensured that copies were sent to the Archive. Throughout our meeting, he addressed all his responses and comments to Eric, whose attentive pose was reminiscent of the famous dog-and-gramophone logo of His Master's Voice.

As we concluded, Obie tilted his head to one side, seemingly checking the dog's opinion of our argument. Eric disdainfully lifted a single ear. Then Obie turned back to us and said, in a bark that turned mid-sentence into a falsetto yelp: 'You have five minutes to take as many CDs off these shelves as you can – and then get the f**k out of my office!' We left without taking a single CD, our tails between our legs.

But several weeks later the flow of releases from PolyGram resumed. For all his gruffness, Obie recognised that his industry's enduring value rested not in the money to be made from the industrial process of making music, but from the cultural contribution it made, and that deserved to be saved for posterity. What he probably didn't realise – after all, almost nobody did at the time – was that his CDs, and the manufacturing and distribution portions of his company's activities, would be consigned to posterity in just a few years' time. The music would endure, but its future was digital.

Jacking in

{'I've Seen That Face Before (Libertango)',
Grace Jones, *Nightclubbing*, 1981}

My first glimpse of this future came in the autumn of 1993, as I sat in the bedroom of my flat in West Hampstead, London and peered at the screen of my Apple PowerBook. By today's standards, the machine was bulky and clunky, made of thick grey plastic with a large rollerball for a mouse. This was the first laptop Apple ever produced; I had just smuggled it in from the United States.

Plugged into the PowerBook was an external spherical camera, housed in a pyramid stand that allowed it to rotate like a chameleon's eye. Cameras like this are built into consumer electronics all the time now, but in the early 1990s this was extraordinary technology, even if it did only manage a low-resolution black and white image. A colour version would take another two years to come out.

On its screen, CUCMe ('see you, see me') software produced large blocks of square pixels that gradually resolved into a series of images from other cameras connected to the internet. It was a mind-blowing breakthrough for the intellectual minority who populated this weird live network. Most participants were academics in places like Stanford, the University of Minnesota and MIT, staring at each other, waving, smiling or looking distractedly in the wrong direction. One night, I noticed I was getting quite a lot of attention and couldn't work out why. Then I realised with amusement and embarrassment that my girlfriend was getting ready for bed and could be seen, over my shoulder, taking off her clothes. For a moment, I had inadvertently become the publisher of a global soft porn channel.

No wonder these guys kept coming back to check out CUCMe. Porn continued to be at the forefront of the digital revolution – replacing top-shelf magazines and seedy movie theatres with content viewable in the privacy of your own home, and developing the commercial infrastructure for online commerce along the way: advertising, marketing, payment and subscription systems. Their successors continued to pioneer – and plague – every subsequent generation of digital communications technology.

My own interest was more chaste. In line with my humanities background, I had always been interested in publishing of the print variety: using ancient technology like Gestetner duplicators to create a poetry magazine and a few short-fiction booklets. The idea of being able to self-publish to whole new audiences, rather than cycle around shops with a butcher's bike full of zines, was appealing in a punky kind of way. That was what had prompted me to get online.

But in the early days of the commercial internet, it was difficult to even *get* online, requiring a complicated and patchy procedure. A modem was plugged into the phone line and dialled into switches, then made a sequence of hissing and sucking noises as it exchanged packets with a distant partner in a kind of digital copulation. When the modem finally connected, it fell silent, probably smoking a digital cigarette in a roseate afterglow in some telephone exchange somewhere. The whole business felt slightly illicit, as if we were doing things that had never been intended to be done over phone lines.[1]

The very difficulty of getting online was part of what made the internet an addictive cult. The complexity of having to dial in, sometimes connecting and sometimes not, gave the internet an air of mystery. Entry could not be taken for granted. Science fiction writer William Gibson had coined the term cyberpunk in his debut novel *Neuromancer* (1984). His work fed the imaginations of early enthusiasts about what the internet could be capable of, and with some amusement my fellow internet enthusiasts and I began to see ourselves as cyberpunks. We were 'jacking in' all the time – the reference to 'jacking up', as junkies did, meant the phrase contained the same memetic combination of addiction, fascination and danger, of accessing something forbidden and life-changing. And whenever we were *not* jacked in, we were impatiently waiting for the next time we would be. If social media has become horribly addictive now, the habit started with the buzz of just getting connected.

Once online, speeds were painfully slow and connections prone to breaking at the worst possible moment. And then you had to figure out where to go. Before 1993, there was no world wide web, no graphical browsers and no search engines. Instead, there were directories of files on computers dotted around the world which could be accessed by a file transfer protocol (FTP). Only a few FTP sites existed, and you had to know their addresses before you could access them. I used to learn about them from listings in *WIRED* magazine, first published in January 1993 – our internet bible at the time.

Many early adopters used a Mac client called Fetch, which featured an animated cartoon terrier running eagerly across the screen, perpetually and enthusiastically chasing a virtual bone.

What he brought back were listings of the contents of university libraries. There were other protocols, too: the University of Minnesota had produced a popular one called Gopher, after the university's mascot. Using it to look at the content of the University of Minnesota library from my bedroom in West Hampstead seemed pretty cool. To download the text of an abstract was mind-blowing, but it took quite a stretch of the imagination to go from these dry offerings to a new entertainment medium.

Nonetheless, the imagination could be so stretched, and as the technology improved, the future entertainment medium became easier to envisage. While I was browsing academic papers, it became obvious that people were also posting other stuff, like music. As I Fetched and Gophered around in late 1993, I found clips by people like Brian Eno, the Future Sound of London and Tangerine Dream. At first the clips only lasted ten seconds. They could have been longer (perhaps as much as thirty seconds) if it hadn't been for the then-glacial speed of file transfer.

The kind of music being posted was an indication of the way in which alternative culture and technological innovation were going hand in hand. Compendium, the famous alternative bookshop where I got my monthly fix of *WIRED*, was the countercultural seed that spawned today's sprawling Camden Market, the largest hipster bazaar in Europe. Back then, it gave us a connection with California, which seemed to be reinventing the future on a monthly basis, often along lines set by the free-thinking successors to the hippies. That was reflected in the branding of early internet service providers: the UK's Demon Internet picked up on the counter-cultural nature of the experience, while the United States' EarthLink had more of a cyber-hippy vibe.

What the post-punk attitudes in the UK and the post-hippy vibes of the United States had in common was an anti-corporate sentiment and a sense that the internet, then uncharted and ungoverned, would liberate ordinary people. The Berlin Wall had fallen just a few years previously, and it felt as though a new era had dawned – one free of the historic constraints and full of potential. Having access to global communications from our bedrooms felt futuristically subversive and strangely empowering, and I felt it deserved to be soundtracked appropriately. And fortunately, I was by then in just the right place to do it – or so I thought.

Working for the man

{'Jarabi', Ketama and Toumani Diabate, *Songhai*, 1988}

In 1988, I moved from the National Sound Archive to work for a stint as a publicity manager at its parent, the British Library. The British Library was in the process of building its new dedicated home on the Euston Road in London and my job was to publicise the benefits of the building to the press and other interested parties. One grandee I showed around the site was John Deacon, then director-general of the British Phonographic Industry. I must have made a favourable impression on him because he suggested that I should come and work for the BPI.

I was to be the acceptable face of the British record industry (although Deacon didn't quite put it like that), which was then catching a lot of flak for selling CDs for far more than their manufacturing cost. That cost was only a small part of the total expense incurred in producing, recording, distributing and marketing records, but that argument wasn't even given the time of day by the media, which was happy to paint the situation as fat-cat record company bosses ripping off ordinary music lovers.[2]

That was not wholly unjustified, because it was indeed an extremely lucrative time to be in the record business. Having invested in promoting compact discs as the flawless and eternal format of the future – a claim that wouldn't hold water even by the end of the 1990s – these were pay-out years for the labels. Many CD collectors were buying music again that they already owned on vinyl, so the record companies were selling music whose costs had long since been recouped or written off. As a result the industry was experiencing a boom in revenues and profits.

This windfall had not gone unnoticed, and so in defending the industry I was ultimately trying to defend the indefensible. It was true that the price of CDs did not reflect the full cost of making music, but also that the industry was making its customers pay over the odds. At one point I ended up on breakfast television, facing off against Neil Tennant of Pet Shop Boys fame. He was serving as the voice of the people; I was the voice of the record companies. He duly wiped the floor with me, and the label bosses were duly furious.

Despite that, I was about to find out what the industry was really like from the inside. I had caught the attention of Paul Conroy, managing director of Virgin Records, after helping to organise the Sound City Festival (subsequently rebranded as Radio 1's long-running Big Weekend roadshow) with BBC Radio 1 and the Musicians' Union. Virgin was reeling from culture shock: having operated as an independent maverick for decades, it had just been acquired by the EMI Group for $1bn. Its big-name acts included the Rolling Stones, Genesis, Phil Collins, Meat Loaf and Janet Jackson; its diverse range of new stars included Massive Attack, the Verve, Smashing Pumpkins and the Spice Girls, as well as a number of the futuristic electronic artists I had found online.

As media affairs director, I found myself working with all layers of the company, and with the ecosystem of artists and managers who mingled in the party atmosphere of Virgin's corporate campus, which spanned the Union Canal off London's Ladbroke Grove. Business-as-usual comprised a mix of laid-back schmoozing and back room deal-making. But to me, it was obvious that what Virgin really needed to do was to get online. Forget the gold discs, the parties, the sex 'n' drugs 'n' rock 'n' roll. Online was where the action *really* was.

It quickly turned out I was just about the only person at Virgin who thought that.

Inasmuch as music executives at the time were aware of the internet at all, it didn't seem like a big deal. If music fans got online and liked it, the executives assumed their labels would eventually make money out of it. The fact that music was ideally suited to the online environment – because its appeal is global, and it is easily digitised – passed them by. Many were more interested in multimedia CD-ROMs – yet another generation of discs that would supposedly fit neatly into the existing way of doing things, and thus enable the labels to make a further killing.

Emboldened by my experience of cyberspace, via my PowerBook and CUCMe, I presented the internet to fellow heads of department at Virgin. I showed them an FTP site on the other side of the planet hosting clips of music by 'our' bands. They were curious for a moment, then amazed at the technology and finally indignant that 'their' music was up there. I told them this was going to change their world. They laughed. When they realised that I was serious, they rolled around laughing and told me I'd been staying up too late.

They were right about that, at least. I couldn't find enough hours in the day to accommodate my fascination for what was unfolding online, and I wasn't alone: the addiction was perceptible in the red-rimmed eyes of my fellow cyberpunks. And what came next got millions more hooked.

The Raft

{'Papua New Guinea', The Future Sound of London, *Accelerator*, 1991}

The internet had emerged out of the US military's desire to create a communications network that would be resistant to nuclear attack – always be able to route around an area that had been knocked out. That made it robust and powerful, but not very user-friendly. Using FTP sites was not much different to hunting around files and folders on your desktop PC, but at arm's length and in the dark.

Tim Berners-Lee, a British scientist working at the CERN research centre near Geneva, had created the concept of the world wide web in 1989, and by 1991 had co-created the first web browser – a program that allowed net addicts to get their fix by typing in addresses and clicking on hyperlinks to visit web pages – far more illuminating than digging through filenames and directory structures.

Despite this revolutionary improvement in usability, the web arrived not with a great fanfare, but with a groan and a stumble. The first browser to be widely used was Mosaic, released by the US National Center for Supercomputing Applications at the University of Illinois in 1993. Its name hinted at its patchwork nature, drawing together different components of text and graphics to make an integrated display. It fell over a lot – and when it did stay up, there still wasn't that much to see.

Netscape Navigator, a more professionally produced product, emerged in November 1994 – the first browser to be widely adopted outside the research community. The company behind it was led by Marc Andreessen and Jim Clark, both of whom went on to become leading Silicon Valley investors. The name Netscape, with its perky logo of an animated letter N stepping over the edge of a planet, suggested the global impact of the new technology, while retaining a cyberpunk edge.

This technology-driven edginess fitted right in with the culture of electronica bands like Daft Punk, the Future Sound of London and Fluke, all signed to Virgin labels in the early 1990s. Building a website to promote them seemed like the obvious response to me. But while Virgin culture happily celebrated the weird, the received wisdom remained that the internet was *too* weird, never going to make it into the mainstream. Fortunately, I suspect Paul Conroy had hired me precisely because I was not the typical music industry type. As a trend-hunter by nature he let me pursue my weird project, even if he had no real idea what it was.

So Virgin's online push was up to me and whatever support I could muster. The musician and writer David Toop introduced me to an early net-head, Paul Sanders, who worked out of the Old Truman Brewery in Brick Lane. (The neighbourhood wasn't trendy back then: just cheap, roomy and damp.) He and his friends were ex-Oxford classicists with an ear for music and a nose for the future. Sanders ran two companies: one called Oscar Music, the other Digital Nomads. We decided to work together right away.[3]

We approached building Europe's first record company website with high ideals. It was an insider medium for a small group who liked to think they were ahead of the curve. This time, we were probably *too* far ahead. True to the countercultural spirit, we did not want any Virgin branding, let alone a hint of corporate EMI. The site was only going to feature a select group of artists who fitted the rave and indie vibe. In the niche naïveté of Web 1.0, the simplest sites and networks were cool: places where anyone could chat and share files, and artists could begin to build relationships with listeners who actually talked back.

We decided we should call it The Raft, inspired by Neal Stephenson's landmark cyberpunk novel *Snow Crash*, in which it was the name for a flotilla of refugee boats surrounding a repurposed aircraft carrier. (*Snow Crash* also featured a seminal depiction of a virtual world, the metaverse, which we all wanted and expected the web to become.) The fictional raft was populated by roving pirates who caused various forms of cyber-havoc – hacking into communications systems and distributing subversive messages, akin to the real world's pirate radio broadcasters. We thought our own Raft would be constructed with equally buccaneering sensibilities in mind.

We had nothing to work with: no computers and no internet connection. We couldn't launch a website with my PowerBook and a 24,000 baud dial-up modem. So we went on a piratical offensive.

Sun Microsystems manufactured the hardcore servers that websites ran on. For Sun, judiciously handing out free computers to emergent web developers made good marketing sense. For all that we felt like we were sowing the seeds of disruption in the music industry, we weren't above taking advantage of its mainstream popularity to saunter into a large corporate office in the city and persuade the marketing department to give us free equipment.

Louise Proddow, our main contact at Sun, was wildly enthusiastic about the web and much happier doing business with some guys from a record label than with her usual corporate customers. So, after some explanations of our plans, we were given a SPARCstation 5 box and a fancy Voyager Unix luggable computer that looked as if it was designed to manage a space mission – and corporate though Sun was, we weren't even asked to put its logo on our website.

Our next task was to get Virgin Records a better connection than the twisted copper pair of the telephone line. Imperial College – whose computing department led the UK in online technology – was in South Kensington, about two miles southeast of the Virgin campus. We discussed our project with the college head of IT. It was an easy negotiation. On hearing our plans, they said we were clearly planning large-scale research into students, the internet and music. We agreed with that description. They said that if we could find someone to make a physical connection between our sites (i.e. lay some cable or a pipe), they would connect us to the superfast joint academic network (SuperJanet) that in turn linked to the backbone of the internet.

Once again, the magic of the music industry cast its spell. Andrew Curry of Videotron, the Canadian company that owned the West London cable franchise, agreed that he needed to give Virgin a high-speed T1 line into its offices because world-famous bands would use his cable network, thus bestowing fame, fortune and fairy dust on all associated with them.[4] While most people felt they were running hot if they had a 56k modem, we were streaming music from some of the best bands in the world at terabytes per second.

We were all set. The Raft launched in the autumn of 1994, at almost exactly the same time as the first version of the Netscape browser. We set up a massive screen in the Virgin boardroom and showed the site off to a hundred or so cheering delegates, from sixty countries, at its annual international conference. We did interviews with the BBC, Channel 4 News and the *Guardian*, who were getting excited about digital innovation. And it was great promotion for the bands, at a lot lower cost than a glossy music video.

For the team at Virgin that was it: a great stunt. But for The Raft team, it established us among a small global elite. Running a music website in the late 1990s was all about subverting the industry. We just weren't sure what would happen next. We were making it up as we went along, waiting with excited anticipation for the next technological breakthrough.

Ahead of the curve

{'My Squelchy Life', Brian Eno, *Nerve Net*, 1992}

It didn't take long for those breakthroughs to arrive. As the web grew, the appetite for new functionality grew with it. The Shockwave platform from Macromedia started to offer 'rich media' experiences inside webpages. Initially we only had 30-second clips of music and a few cool animated graphics, but before long we were running webcasts and video streams, and inviting artists to join online chats, creating new kinds of bonds between the lives of the bands and their fans. It was clear that we could create more intimate communities online than would ever be possible in 'real life', which has continued to be true with every subsequent iteration of online life.

We uploaded everything we could to the website: in one series of editorial features, we asked artists to come in and empty their pockets, then scanned the contents (which always seemed to include packets of Rizla cigarette rolling papers and little bits of cardboard). We became equally addicted to telling stories on the web and to finding new ways to play with the technology to engage our audience. There was scope to create narratives and experiences that were again unlike anything we could do through conventional media.

Some of the potential breakthroughs were before their time. For example, all this activity produced data – tons of it. Big data, and the degree to which our world is informed and shaped by it, is now a cliché: companies of all kinds make use of highly sophisticated techniques to track and analyse traffic across the web, with the aim of anticipating potential customers' behaviour and marketing to them accordingly. It's this information and analysis that have propelled the development of the modern web and social media, and that might have demonstrated the value of our pioneering website to sceptics like the powers-at-be at Virgin.

The Raft attracted visitors from all over the globe: we wanted to know how people found it, which pages were popular and which weren't, and which countries visitors were from. We wanted to be able to tell our international marketing folk where in the world different artists were popular on the internet. But all we had were raw data logs generated by our servers, which we duly circulated, but we wanted to get a sense of it in real time.

I set our IT team to try and come up with a statistical analysis programme that could follow users through the sites and visualise their movements in real time. We had a notion that we could have 'web jockeys' who could change the content of pages according to what was popular or trending, and do deals with other sites as we learned where people came from and where they went after they left us. The principle was sound: that's how the online advertising ecosystem works today, albeit the jockeys are algorithms rather than humans, brokering adverts and links from cookies data, second to second.

It took the IT team a year to work out that they didn't have a machine anywhere near powerful enough to process all the data that the website produced. They also realised that they had nothing big enough to store the data, even if they could begin to find a way of processing it. What we were seeing was the potential for online marketing, but that would take far more computing power than a music company could muster. It wasn't until a decade later that I ended up at a company capable of attacking this problem, to say nothing of the even larger quantities of data hauled off today's web and social media combined.

The Raft kept operating for years, long after I had moved on. Over time, its idealism was tempered somewhat – it began to include EMI's roster as well Virgin's more cutting-edge acts – but its direct connection between artists and listeners continued to challenge the way record companies worked. The major labels continued to focus their marketing spends on getting other companies – broadcasters, retailers and so on – to promote their music, rather than on reaching fans directly. If they wanted to create the appearance of street credibility, they would spend some money on illegal flyposting. To paste posters up in London's fly-posting sites, you had to deal with a gentleman called Terry the Pill: if you posted without paying him, he would break your knees. That was what made it 'edgy'.

The labels also remained convinced that their product would remain firmly physical. A music company like EMI was equipped to manufacture, distribute and retail round bits of plastic in shiny boxes. Innovation had consisted of making discs first out of shellac, then vinyl and eventually aluminium-coated polycarbonate. To that end, fortunes were squandered on futile attempts to find a successor to CDs: multimedia discs, playable in the increasing number of home computers fitted with CD-ROM drives; Sony's MiniDisc, a handy portable format; DVD-Audio, designed to offer ultimate fidelity of sound and vision. All of them were doomed.

As this was going on, the internet kept getting more and more addictive. Every time we jacked in, some new capability had appeared, some new digital territory had been colonised. We could operate a crane in a sandpit on the other side of the world. We could dress up as avatars that would appear on other people's screens. We could send messages on chat channels open to the world. We could see web traffic flowing in from countries all over the world. Information, connection, liberation: our cyberpunk fantasies were coming to life with every click.

Entrepreneurs outside the recording industry had recognised that music was the perfect gateway drug for those who had yet to develop an internet addiction, and that the record companies were doing next to nothing to capitalise on that. The mid-1990s saw a plethora of experiments with digital music distribution, from services that would let you create a personalised CD while you shopped for jeans to what we would now call streaming services. But most of these were doomed too – not because they were bad ideas, but because the technology usually wasn't ready, wasn't developed enough, the audience often wasn't ready and most of all because the labels weren't anywhere near ready. For any of these services to work, they needed music – and at that time the labels simply didn't see any point in providing it. That was a massive missed opportunity, as would later become painfully apparent.

For my part, still firmly ensconced within EMI in London,

I fantasised about webcasting recording sessions from Abbey Road Studios, or allowing fans to be involved in the making of their favourite artists' creations. In the event, what I managed to do was get EMI's four London locations hooked up to a high-bandwidth ring, which made it cheaper and easier to move master recording files around. Useful enough, but a long way from the cyberpunk visions I had been nurturing – and conversations with the top brass at EMI made it clear that those visions would remain just that. Visions.

My inability to make my own company appreciate that the web represented more than a peripheral stunt, even after the pioneering success of The Raft, was immensely frustrating. It might have been only one small piece of the early web, but its development signalled to me the heady mix of addiction and entrepreneurialism that characterised the online world and those building it. That stood in stark contrast to the complacent attitude I saw in the rest of the music industry – a complacency that I was to see again and again as the digital revolution swept over many other old-guard industries.

In fact, my experience with The Raft signalled all the factors that contributed to the making of the digital world we know today. There was the liberatory potential of the internet, and its ability to connect people – in this case, musicians and fans – in new and exciting ways. There was the ease of sharing digital information, which posed a radical threat to business as usual. There was the substitution of physical commodities with digital assets, and the importance of securing a community to support them. There was the potential for creators to take power back from the intermediaries, and for new types of company to exploit the vast quantities of data created by online activity to forge new relationships with customers. At the time, our favourite term was 'disintermediate' – cutting out the middleman. What of course we were really doing was simply paving the way for the insertion of entirely new middlemen (and they were mostly men).

As we'll see, all these factors came into play over the course of the digital revolution – albeit they didn't necessarily play out the way I optimistically anticipated at the outset. Nor would it have been easy to articulate them back at the dawn of the consumer web: I list them here with the benefit of hindsight. But at the time, it seemed clear to me that a new world was being made, one built with a punkish, anything-goes ethos and little regard for tradition – exactly the kind of attitude labels like Virgin had once epitomised. If I wanted to be part of this new world – and I did – there was only one place to be: among the pioneers and pirates of the digital frontier, in the wild west of Silicon Valley.

2

DOTCOM REVOLUTION

{'Teardrop', Massive Attack, *Mezzanine*, 1998}

One dingy November afternoon in 1996, Larry Miller of AT&T Labs walked into my office, holding a clunky-looking black box – the chassis of an old Sony Walkman CD player, held together with duct tape. But the guts of the CD player had been removed: no rotor, no laser head, not even a door to put the disc in. In fact, Miller's device had no moving parts at all. It was the world's first ever mp3 player.

Miller was on a mission. He was an evangelist for mp3, a new format for digital music that had been jointly patented by AT&T, the Fraunhofer Institute in Germany, Thomson-CSF and France Telecom. The standard had been released in 1993, the same year as the Mosaic web browser, and these two technologies together made it possible to create a music file small enough to be offered for quick and easy download to anyone, anywhere in the world.

Websites spread like wildfire all over the internet, many of them offering clips of music to download in mp3 format – legally or otherwise. What Miller was offering was the final piece of the digital music puzzle: portability. A generation of music lovers had grown up expecting to soundtrack their lives, thanks to Sony's revolutionary Walkman, which first used cassettes and then CDs. Now they could use a digital player – even more lightweight and capacious – to do the same. I immediately wanted one: it was clearly genius.

What Miller's box offered in functionality, it lacked in style. Of course, this was simply a laboratory prototype, a proof of concept. In the event, AT&T never turned it into an actual product: it seemed too far from its core business.[1] It was two years before the launch of the first consumer mp3 player. The Diamond Rio was a small black box with a tiny monochrome screen, about the size of a pack of cards: it sat comfortably in the palm of my hand. A cable connected the Rio to a desktop computer and some simple software allowed files to be transferred.

If you *had* the files. The music industry was still reluctant to provide them – but by some oversight, there was no copy protection in the 'Red Book' audio CD standard, created by Sony and Philips in the early 1980s. That meant that ripping CDs to create mp3 files that could be put on a player was fairly straightforward, although many people skipped that stage altogether and simply downloaded the files they wanted from the internet. The first edition of the Rio went on to sell more than 200,000 units – not bad for a novel, pricey and largely unsupported device.

In 1997, Californian entrepreneur Michael Robertson tapped into this demand with the launch of MP3.com, a simple, if idealistic, website that allowed any band, however famous or obscure, to post mp3s of its tracks. Consumers could surf the site, browse the newest or most popular tracks, download and listen to them. On the face of it, MP3.com just looked like a new way of marketing bands. But a whole new kind of business emerged from it: a platform that enabled artists to reach out to their customers directly.

Robertson built a huge cult following, showing up at the rapidly growing calendar of digital music conferences and laying into the Luddite, fan-unfriendly music industry with a witty and campaigning spirit. His free-market attitude, customer focus and persistent desire to disrupt the music industry kept him pursuing new features – new ways in which the combination of the web and mp3 could be made more attractive. He became the hero of the mp3 nation.

The labels reacted to all this with suspicion and hostility. The definition of a major label was that it ran its own manufacturing and controlled its own distribution. The conspiring technologies of mp3 and the web did away with both those key components at a stroke: they stabbed directly at the heart of the majors. They turned to their own weapon of choice: the courts. In 1998, the Recording Industry Association of America (RIAA) sued to have the Rio banned, arguing that its existence was an incitement to copyright infringement. The case failed, the judge ruling that the device allowed its users to move their music around, not to copy it illegally.

At this point, the music industry, finally sensing a threat to its dominance, belatedly started to develop alternatives. There was a narrow window of opportunity, because mp3's position was not yet unassailable. But the labels' attempts to create alternatives floundered. Standards proliferated, with unmemorable names like AAC, AACR2, OGG Vorbis, FLAC and Windows Media Audio (WMA). They were clunky to use and encumbered by copy-protection systems.

There were also doomed attempts in the late 1990s to create a cross-industry standard for digital music distribution, under portentous names like the Madison Project and the Secure Digital Music Initiative. Meetings were held in agreeably romantic locations around the world – Kyoto, Hawaii, Florence and London – and were a curious combination of academic indulgence, music biz luxury and sharp-elbowed deal-making.

Technologists were invited to participate, including both

giant infrastructure firms like IBM and ambitious dotcom start-ups with bright ideas and piles of investors' cash to burn through. The contrast between these two tribes was striking, to put it mildly. The label guys swaggered in wearing jeans and T-shirts under sports jackets. A few of the men still wore ponytails. The tech guys were in blue shirts and beige chinos with highly polished black shoes.

But the labels couldn't agree on anything: digital rights management, transaction mechanisms, audio compression quality and choice, end playback systems, device control, CD-burning capabilities: the list went on, and so did the arguments. The disruptive complexities of internet commerce arose persistently and inevitably. How could you divide up the revenues if a recording of a performance of a piece of music belonged to a UK record label, but was sold from a French website to a US tourist using a Canadian credit card? While the labels argued about who should get paid, their erstwhile customers and the upstart technologists had come up with a radical new answer: no one.

Time to take my shot

{'Wake Up', Rage Against the Machine, 1992}

While all this was going on, I had wangled a transfer to the West Coast – not to Silicon Valley, but to the iconic 'stack-of-records' Capitol Records Building at the corner of Hollywood and Vine in Los Angeles. Like an increasing number of younger execs in the music business, I felt conflicted about the fast-growing digital music scene. On the one hand, I had an obligation to adhere to my employer's approach. On the other hand, I felt that change and innovation should be as natural to the creative industries as to the creators themselves. I hoped my role as EMI's liaison to the exciting new dotcom world would let me find a way to bridge the divide.

It didn't take long for me to be disabused of that notion. The entrance hall was lined with signed black-and-white photographs of Frank Sinatra, Dean Martin and the rest of the Brat Pack, who had all recorded in the building's famous basement studio. The previous occupant of my ninth-floor office had been the company's financial controller: as the new media guy, there was something of a question mark as to where I belonged – if anywhere. And four floors above me was the office of former Capitol head honcho Gary Gersh, now permanently closed – as if it were some sort of shrine to past glory days.

It soon became apparent that the only thing EMI wanted from the dotcoms was their money. The Valley was awash with both cash and ideas. The dotcom dream was to get your idea funded, grow as quickly as possible and then make an initial public offering (IPO) of stock at a colossal valuation. When a hotly tipped stock went public, the volume of trading could be immense and the value of shares could be highly volatile, reaching hugely inflated levels that had nothing to do with the commercial performance of the company – profits, or even revenues, were a more-or-less optional extra a lot of the time – but play it right and this kind of IPO volatility would make founders, investors and investment bankers immensely rich.

The music industry saw no reason it shouldn't get in on this action. Not by embracing these new ideas, but by licensing music to the entrepreneurs who needed it to build their ideas: streaming and subscription services, a-la-carte downloads, rent-to-buy, in-store kiosks where you could burn your own CDs or fill up your mp3 player, hulking hard drives containing all the world's music in a single box and matchboxes with a speaker that could play just a single track. For a while, it even looked as though ringtones might be the future of the music industry.

EMI's attitude was to soak these entrepreneurs for as much cash as possible, in keeping with the adage that the people who had really made money from the gold rush were not the miners but the people who sold them picks and shovels. While the technologists thought they were about to turn the music industry upside down, the industry was quietly confident it could prevent that happening – and for a while, it was proven correct.

'Supplicants' were afforded a warm welcome – and a genuine one, inasmuch as people like me (there were one or two in every label) were genuinely interested in what the technologists had come up with. But that was generally the precursor to a savage stitch-up on the deal terms, usually including a huge cash advance, a healthy share of revenues and a hefty chunk of the dotcom's shares. This kind of licensing netted the labels millions of dollars. For the labels it was like taking candy from children.

Until two of those children of the dotcom age decided not to play by the rules. In June 1999, Sean Parker and Shawn Fanning launched Napster, a free-to-use service that allowed people to share files with each other directly. Immediately and eagerly adopted by music fans, it was the first widely used peer-to-peer (P2P) network. The vision was not so different from the ones that had been circulating in the Valley for a while, but with one crucial difference: on Napster, no one was paying for the music. And no one – neither the artists, nor the music publisher, nor the labels – was getting paid for it.

Napster offered the entire world's music collection – for free. It was both more comprehensive than any record store could ever be, or even than the labels collectively could have been, with unpublished and bootleg recordings sitting alongside unofficial duplicates of official releases. It literally unleashed music from corporate control, allowing killer tracks to be divorced from album fillers, and spawned a whole new generation of ideas about how to access music. For once, it is no exaggeration to say that it changed the world.

Almost overnight, Napster put the major labels on the ropes. They responded the only way they knew how: with a lawsuit. This time, their justification was clear: Napster really did directly facilitate blatant copyright infringement on an unprecedented scale. Of course, a simpler, if more galling, answer was staring them in the face. Napster had the potential to create immense new audiences and new revenues, via a subscription fee – essentially the same model that Spotify would deploy successfully twenty years later.[2]

Napster was the final straw for me. By late 1999, my own discomfort at working in a label had grown unbearable. Job offers from audacious, entrepreneurial outfits were looking more attractive than continuing to try to make the corporation genuinely commit to the kinds of innovation that were coming across my desk every day. I was not alone: as IPOs became more and more crazily valued towards the end of the millennium, promising overnight riches, experienced folk were increasingly swapping their corporate salaries for start-up equity. But taking the step to leave the safety of a large company, with its guaranteed salary, benefits and bonuses was still very scary when it really came to it.

Most of the offers that came my way were obvious nonstarters, based on assumptions about how the music industry worked that would never have flown. But one stood out precisely because it came from two good engineers who knew they didn't understand the business, but wanted to: Toni Schneider, a Swiss-German who had emigrated to San Francisco five years earlier, and Mike Taylor who had come to the Valley from Columbus, Ohio. They had great technology company pedigrees and business development brains, and they were willing to go the distance to get me on board. And so it was that we formed Uplister, Inc., headquartered in San Francisco, California.

A brush with the law

{'Watching the Detectives', Elvis Costello,
My Aim is True, 1977}

Uplister was founded on the assumption that the new unit of music consumption was not the album but the playlist. With all the world's music now fragmented into individual tracks, and the constraints of physical media rapidly fading into history, there was no need for 'the product' to be an arbitrary, but fixed, collection of tracks. We believed people would pay for searchable and shareable playlists curated by fellow music lovers.[3]

We also enriched the original concept of a playlist from a simple listing to something more narrative and visual, containing text and graphics. We encouraged people to tell stories about the music: the history of a band or a genre, why that music was important to that person, or just compile a great sequence for a workout. People created their playlists and then uploaded them.

The idea was sound, but our timing was bad. As I was waiting for my new, EMI-free visa to be granted, word came that the wildly inflated bubble in dotcoms had finally burst. I got my visa, but by April 2000 hundreds of companies had gone bust, thousands of people had lost their jobs and investors had lost millions, if not billions, of dollars. But our own backer, Andy Rappaport of August Capital, remained optimistic, albeit that he invested only a comparatively modest $6m in Uplister (although it seemed like a lot more back then).

For me though, entering the start-up world was just exhilarating. I finally regained the intoxication I had felt when making my first forays into cyberspace, and then again when building The Raft. The learning curve was intense, but instead of worrying about which corporate rival might try to stab me in the back, I spent my time focused on ways to make our service more attractive and fervently promoting to anyone who cared to listen, the future vision that we were developing together. We built a great team of thirty-five developers and marketeers. It was a relaxed, collegiate environment: the whole team would go out after work to karaoke bars, or play ball games against other dotcoms in the neighbourhood.

Unfortunately, the good vibes didn't translate into a sustainable business. As we went out to try to raise more investment we came across a wall of rejection: investors were running scared of anything that looked too innovative. We could only license a few independent labels for the music we needed to make our service work, as the majors were still trying to rip off dotcoms for all they were worth. As things got more intense, we approached Napster to see if a partnership could be struck.

We contemplated taking a leaf out of Napster's book. If it could use music without a licence, why couldn't we? There were other file-sharing services, notably Gnutella, which had no central server and thus, in theory, no weak spot for a legal attack. We duly hooked Uplister up to Gnutella. Suddenly all the text-only playlists our thousands of users had created lit up with the audio. We didn't have to limp along with thirty-second clips or offer only the patchy selections of music we had managed to license. It was dazzling.

We knew that if we put the product out, we would become

heroes to the burgeoning online music community. We also knew that if we put it out, we would be toast. The labels would sue in the blink of an eye and the venture capitalists would have an unbeatable reason not to get involved. Rappaport encouraged us to keep up the momentum and extended another $2m to keep us going. Pedal to the metal, he said, but nobody else would touch us with a bargepole.

We contemplated turning the Gnutella functionality on anyway – we called the new product Swizzler. Napster had gone public with an equally scofflaw product, and although it had legal troubles, it still seemed to be on course to fame and fortune. What did we have to lose?

I was about to find out. One day, my deliberations were interrupted by an unexpected phone call from the RIAA. I was to be deposed by lawyers acting for Michael Robertson, founder of MP3.com. Robertson, like Fanning and Parker, was a hero to the dot-commers and a villain to the music industry. At its peak, MP3.com delivered more than four million mp3 audio files per day to over 800,000 unique users, with a customer base of 25 million registered users; its July 1999 IPO had been the most profitable ever.

Robertson was continually adding clever functionality to his site. In 2000 he added a feature called Beam-it, which allowed consumers who had bought a CD to upload its tracks to a digital locker and then stream it over the internet to their preferred device, whatever it happened to be, and wherever they happened to be. Another feature, Instant Listening, gave users access to the music on a CD as soon as they registered it with the site. To the majors these looked like clear tests of their tolerance, and they duly sued.

I'm sure Robertson had me deposed because he knew I had jumped the fence and would be sympathetic to his project.

But as a former executive, I was under an obligation to EMI to continue to toe the company line that file-sharing was bad and immoral. I was in effect betting that online music was the future even as I had to profess, on behalf of my former employer, that it wasn't. I had even made a rare personal investment in Loudeye, a cloud-based media storage service – which, as luck would have it, was going public on the same day as my deposition.

It was an unpleasant and fraught experience. A deposition can last from six to twelve hours, and in this case Robertson's lawyers were asking probing questions about my personal music habits, in the hope that I would slip up and reveal that file-sharing was not the sin the labels said it was. Had I ever ripped a CD to mp3? How might I go about doing that? Would it be fair for others to? I gave non-committal answers in a monotone.

Over lunch, I learned from my wife that we had netted a few thousand dollars when we sold off our Loudeye shares – something that the MP3.com lawyers might have already suspected, since I had unwisely asked how its IPO was going during an earlier break. That afternoon, one of them asked me if I was an investor in any digital music company other than Uplister. I was able to reply, pedantically but truthfully, that I was not, because I had just sold my shares.

It was a heart-stopping moment. Had he phrased his question differently, I would have had to disclose the investment, and that would probably have led to a starring role in the main trial. As it was, I bored them into submission and there was no follow up.

After the experience of the deposition, I had zero appetite for that – and little appetite for skirting the law with Uplister. As it turned out, both Napster and MP3.com eventually lost their cases and ironically were sold to the labels that let them wither away, although their founders still enjoyed some financial upside from the sales. Uplister, by contrast, limped on for a little longer before we finally decided to close the company, let our staff go and pay off our creditors. Not an easy way to finish such an ambitious project, but we learned enormously from our experience and Toni Schneider went on to become the CEO of Automattic, the company behind WordPress.

I never regretted my decision to give a start-up a go, though. I had got into all of this because I believed the internet could make the distribution of music slicker and more enjoyable for both artists and fans. I was interested in its disruptive potential, but not to the extent that I wanted to make it impossible for artists to make a living. Clearly the people at Napster felt differently about what they were doing: their willingness to put what was technically possible ahead of what was socially acceptable set the template for much of what was to follow. I'm not sure if there is a direct lineage but certainly the disrupt at all costs attitude, the famous invocation to 'break things', ultimately led to the corporate cultures of both Facebook and Uber. Back in the old world though, the music industry's love of litigation was about to lead to its downfall.

You wouldn't steal a car

{'Nagoya Marimbas', Steve Reich, *Striking a Balance*, 1998}

It is an unspoken rule of business – unspoken probably because no one ever felt it necessary to say it – that declaring war on a large proportion of your potential customers is rarely a route to commercial success. Yet, through its anger and frustration at technological change and its addiction to aggressive litigation, that is exactly what the music industry spent the first decade of the twenty-first century doing.

The dotcom boom and bust had provided a period of respite for the record labels. They had milked dotcoms during the boom, and then ignored them during the bust. Napster and MP3.com were being sued into oblivion. But file-sharing hadn't gone away. Numerous other services – Gnutella, Kazaa, Grokster, LimeWire and BitTorrent – had popped up to fill the void. The music industry's narrative was that file-sharing was the single greatest challenge to its business model. Loss of control of manufacturing, distribution and retail is not mentioned in that narrative. The effect was to make the industry look more Luddite than it actually is.

But it is a fact that if music can be played back via digital technology, it can be copied and shared. Ultimately, digital rights management doesn't work and creating technical friction around files simply created a commercial friction too. At that point, without a ready technological fix, and having failed to build their own alternatives, the labels had no option but to turn to the law.

But this was problematic too. The new services were designed to have no central server or corporate owner that could be targeted with a lawsuit, or were based in jurisdictions that were unlikely to enforce a court ruling made in London or Los Angeles. So, if the industry couldn't shut the services down, perhaps it could 'persuade' people not to use them?

So began the RIAA's Project Hubcap, whose nondescript name possibly derived from the idea that it was targeting 'street kids' who also participated in the hip-hop-inspired fashion of stealing hubcaps and brand mascots from parked cars. The industry was keen to equate file-sharing with other theft – hence the infamous 'You wouldn't steal a car' advertisement. And it went to some lengths to associate file-sharing with piracy, even though a file-sharer was vastly more likely to be a computer nerd with a fat server and a fast connection than a hardened criminal.

The messaging didn't work, and so the music industry decided to take firmer action: it started to sue listeners. Between 2003 and 2009, the music industry initiated over 30,000 lawsuits in the United States alone, citing copyright infringement using peer-to-peer networks. By applying pressure to friendly politicians and internet providers, the file-sharers found themselves facing penalties including enormous fines, suspension of internet access and even jail time.

Despite the industry's claim to be going after hardened pirates and cyber-criminals, the objects of Project Hubcap's wrath turned out to include children, students, the elderly and even the recently deceased. Even this huge number of writs was not enough to make a dent in file-sharing – but through the associated publicity, the aim was to teach people that this is a serious offence. As an education programme it certainly had an impact: it taught people to loathe and fear the music industry. Stories abounded of hapless 'first offenders' terrified by the abrupt threat of prison, or parents saddled with huge fines racked up by their errant kids.

The industry argued that file-sharing was theft, costing musicians their livelihoods; file-sharing advocates pointed out that copying a digital file wasn't anything like stealing a physical possession and claimed most of the files shared would never have been purchased anyway. It might even help, by allowing people to discover and sample artists they would never otherwise have encountered, and the labels were operating as a 'corrupt cartel', refusing to cut a deal that would allow the fruits of the new technology to be enjoyed. The labels retorted with equal disdain that far from being fans, the downloaders were just 'freetards' who expected to get away without paying for the fruits of others' labour. And so on.

Whatever the merits (or otherwise) of the industry's arguments, Project Hubcap came across as harsh and impersonal corporate aggression rather than a defence of music and its creators. A more effective negative public relations campaign could not have been orchestrated. It drove an immense wedge between the labels and fans, creating a rift that has still not been repaired, and that probably paved the way for other, less compromised brands to muscle in on digital music. And they soon did.

The Trojan horse

{'Yamore', Salif Keita and Cesaria Evora, *Mofou*, 2002}

The year 2001 was just a few days old when Apple announced iTunes, which combined a download store, CD ripping and media library management in a user-friendly package. Later that year, it announced the iPod, an intuitive, stylish gadget that let you carry a hitherto unimaginable number of songs in your pocket. The hardware–software combination finally achieved what no one had previously managed: a legal, convenient solution for digital music.

The response was immediate, delirious excitement. In just a few years, Apple became the mightiest player in digital music. The story has been told well elsewhere,[4] so I won't repeat it at length here. Apple co-founder Steve Jobs, who had regained control of the company in 1996, had spent years positioning its devices as the natural tools of the creative industries, as well as sponsoring experiments in interactive media.

Perhaps that was why the labels listened to him when he told them that iTunes was the solution they had been looking for. Reeling from the onslaught of Napster, the labels agreed to sell their music at a flat 99 cents per track, with copy protection, rather than full albums. Perhaps they didn't think too hard about what they were signing away. But it soon became apparent that music buyers were quite happy to buy individual tracks, and that the returns to record labels would be nothing like that earned on CDs.

And it soon became even more obvious that Apple, not the record labels, was in control of the pricing and distribution of online music – and that it had no interest in preserving the labels' profit margins. Like so many other technology companies, it had recognised that music was a useful entry point for consumers – in this case, consumers who would buy its sleek, expensive hardware.

The record industry's revenues plummeted, and the labels' share prices tumbled even as Apple's soared. By 2007, Apple was undoubtedly calling the shots: when Jobs demanded that the labels drop copy protection, in the service of smoother consumer experience, they had little choice but to comply. The balance of power between the music business and the technology industry had finally flipped: Apple needed the labels, but not as much as the labels needed Apple. They had finally been overthrown not by their declared foes in the start-up sector, but by a major power that had, in iTunes, assembled a Trojan horse which allowed it to first get inside the industry's defences and then to overrun it from within.

There's a deeper lesson to be drawn from the fate of the record labels, though. Apple won not through technological innovation (although it used that) or commercial nous (although Jobs had that), but because it gave music fans what they wanted: convenient, portable access to all the music they could ever want.

That was something the music industry had refused to do not just for the decade of the digital revolution, but for the half-century preceding it. During the analogue era, people could listen to the radio for free (and what they heard was heavily influenced and sometimes directly controlled by the labels);[5] or they could buy a record, either paying over the odds for a single track or forking out for an album often padded out with tracks that were less commercial or even good. That mentality persisted even as a world emerged in which people could listen to almost anything they wanted to, whenever they wanted to – and for that matter, paying for it only if they wanted to. It was literally a free-for-all.

And what they wanted to listen to wasn't necessarily what the record companies wanted them to listen to. Given infinite online music libraries, many people returned to music they had enjoyed years or decades earlier. Younger people, previously the most engaged consumers of recorded music, were also increasingly distracted by other things, like games, videos and social media. Music was fighting for attention with everything else available on the internet, and in many cases, ended up as merely the soundtrack to something more compelling.

It didn't help that the industry's actual product was no longer remotely appealing. Vinyl LPs were at the heart of a cultural experience that was broader than the music alone. A band's intent was to be deciphered from the graphics, the design, the sleeve notes or from half-readable words etched into the inner grooves of the vinyl. Records came in coloured vinyl or on picture discs; in elaborate packaging with posters and gatefold covers; and could be played in unorthodox ways by DJs and turntablists. Hard core music fans, or musos as we liked to call them, could enjoy reading details of who played what instrument on which tracks and who the session musicians were; fans could admire glossy shots of their idols and speculate about their love lives; conspiracists could discuss the messages hidden in cryptic artwork and backwards recorded vocals. Even the purchasing process – queuing up on the day of release or rifling through crates for rarities – added to the excitement and the mystique.

A track downloaded from a file-sharing network, on the other hand, often lacked even accurate metadata about the artist and release. It was a commodity designed to play a strictly functional role. iTunes has to take a large share of the blame here: its anodyne appearance, simple functionality and comprehensiveness no doubt contributed to its popularity, but utterly eradicated any vibe or cultural context there might have been. Spotify has made attempts to polish up its interface – embracing the kind of playlist functionality we pioneered at Uplister – but is still pretty much a searchable database and still doesn't tell you who the members of every band were or who played what instruments on which tracks.

Similar patterns were to recur in other industries: complacency about the competitive threat; disorganised responses that tried to cling to the old ways of doing things; an inability to update their ideas about what customers, suppliers and workers wanted; and extreme difficulty creating attractive digital equivalents or replacements for their existing products and services.

It was more often the technologists who found it easier to respond to these challenges. They preferred experiment to experience, were building from scratch rather than trying to rebuild existing businesses, and often had lots of money to throw at a problem and weren't too worried about whether their activities were strictly legal or ethical. But stripped of all values except the profit motive, there was plenty of scope for them to develop problems of their own: exploitative labour practices, appropriation of others' work, and contribution to social division and toxic environments.

I was to see all this in my subsequent career, and it was to cement my belief that a 'good' business had to mean more than one that simply grew as fast as possible and made money by any means possible. Because the digital revolution had only just started.

3

CREATIVE COMMUNITIES

{*Variations on a Theme of Frank Bridge,* Benjamin
Britten and the English Chamber Orchestra, 1969}

I first met Ben and Jonathan Finn in a restaurant. True to
expectations of identical twins, they both independently
ordered exactly the same meal from the extensive menu. They
met the stereotype in other ways too: for example, they'd
sometimes turn up to work wearing the same clothes. They
didn't need to finish each other's sentences, because they both
already knew what the end of the sentence was going to be.
Talking to them was delightful, baffling and at times exasper-
ating, as they often seemed to inhabit a knowledge bubble in
which all was entirely clear to them, but simply not obvious to
anyone outside.

This was added to by the fact that they are both extraordi-
narily bright. While studying music at school, they had learned
that most scores were still created by one of a few laborious
methods: copied by hand, engraved into printing plates, or
using stick-on transfers. As they were also interested in computers, the solution seemed obvious, but it turned out to be
tough to crack. Nonetheless, they persisted through their
university years and by the time they graduated they had a
working 'scorewriter' program: basically a word processor for
musical notation. Why they called it Sibelius neither claims to

remember: perhaps it was simply because the famous composer of that name was also a Finn.

The Finns initially tried to get music publishers to distribute their software – but they proved just as myopic as the labels. So the brothers started approaching composers directly, who leapt at the opportunity to automate their working practices. A composer using Sibelius could edit his or her score and create copies suitable for professional use, make arrangements for different instruments and produce the parts for players to use in sessions just by pressing a button.

In 1993, the brothers set up their own business, with Jonathan looking after the technology and Ben taking care of the sales and marketing. They offered not just the software, but the hardware too: most composers at the time didn't have a computer, printer or electronic keyboard. It didn't come cheap. The full package cost up to £4,000, and two years later Sibelius was turning over £500,000, having become the standard for serious musicians.

For the rest of the 1990s, Sibelius continued to thrive. The original product ran on the Acorn computers common in British educational and domestic use, but little known worldwide; so the company developed a version for Windows, which had proved hugely successful, and continued to roll out new features. By the time I came across the company, it was the UK leader in this narrow but sizeable and growing market: an impressive product with an incredible reputation. The company had grown to thirty-five people split into two teams: sales and marketing in Cambridge; and development in an attic office near Waterloo Station in London.

When I met them in 2002, the Finns fairly soon confided in me that they wanted out. They had spent all their adult lives on this product, and as young, smart and ambitious men they wanted to do something else with the remainder of their lives – and, I sensed, something that would disentangle their destinies: despite (or perhaps because of) their closeness, the brothers preferred to work in separate offices. The business had been a huge commercial, creative and emotional investment for them both, and now the time had come to realise its value.

That meant the business was also an enormous liability for the brothers: they had seen the dotcom bust and were worried about what might happen to their life's work. They would have liked to sell up, but 2002 was a year in which anyone running a start-up was fully occupied just trying to keep it up and running. Even if a buyer could be found, any valuation was likely to be depressed. So for the moment, the business had to keep moving forward; as a system built around desktop computers, that meant coming up with a way to address the increasingly obvious opportunity – and threat – of the internet. And that was where I came in.

Stepping up to the plate

{'Blue Train', John Coltrane, *Blue Train*, 1958}

Sibelius was a lovely company; not one but two genius founders and a team full of dedication, passion and a belief in the importance and value of the product. When I arrived, it was still run in quite an ad hoc fashion and part of the board's expectation was that I would in some ways professionalise the business. Coming fresh from the hallowed portals of Silicon Valley, it was an interesting challenge. Here was a successful company that had made pioneering use of technology, but that nonetheless needed to take more steps towards a fully digital existence. After all, its products were still shipped in expensive cardboard boxes, with shrink-wrapped discs to run on desktop computers, and it was already clear that was not the future. The two founders had invested all their adult lives into building the business and were keen to reduce their exposure by seeking some kind of sale.

So for three months I worked with them as an adviser to work out how to get the business into shape. It was an interesting problem, although working with the Finns could be challenging. They understood everything about what the other one was thinking but didn't always understand why other people couldn't understand what they were talking about. That made for a fascinating but complicated dynamic, one that I learned to navigate with the assistance of Alison Kerr, who had worked with Ben and Jonathan for several years before I arrived.

Alison had previously worked in Formula 1 racing, and then for the Saatchi brothers, so her skills in marketing and PR were outstanding, but her overall management skills were even stronger. She recognised that the company needed to develop its strategy, and that required it to bring in some new experience from outside – so she, the brothers Finn and the chairman, Sir Colin Southgate, set about looking for a CEO. (Southgate, as chairman of Thorn EMI, had previously read me the riot act when I had inadvertently hinted to the *Financial Times* in 1996 that EMI was interested in distributing music over a French cable network. It wasn't.)

By the end of three months strategising around Sibelius, we had a plan of action. I really thought I could help even though it was nothing like any business I'd worked in before, but we all worked well together. So it was no great surprise when the Finns asked me to stay on and see the plan through as CEO. It was a significant step: I had been in senior executive positions for many years, and played a leadership role at Uplister, but this would be the first time that the buck would stop with me. I was very conscious of not just the strategic and financial responsibility I would be taking on, but the attendant responsibility to the Sibelius team and the community of Sibelius users.

Uplister had, by my reckoning, been something of a victim of circumstance. Had the dotcom crash not happened, we would have had a good chance of going back to investors for the money we needed for comprehensive licensing deals. It hadn't turned out that way. But getting Uplister up and running had been like the most concentrated MBA course imaginable. My co-founders and I had gained an incredible sense of how to make the elements of a technology-driven business work together: how to run a software development team, how to build up a business and how to talk to investors and other stakeholders. I felt ready for the challenge.

From Finsbury Park to the world

{'Games People Play', King Curtis, *Instant Groove*, 1969}

My first job was to merge the offices. The teams were arguably in the wrong places – sales and marketing would more logically be in London, and the devs in Cambridge. But more fundamentally, the team was too small to be split over two locations. We found a new office close to Finsbury Park station, which was handily on the Cambridge train line. We announced the move to the staff with some trepidation: would the sales team accept a much longer commute?

As it turned out, the sales and marketing people were delighted to have an excuse to hang out in the Big Smoke. Instead, it was the devs, who were being asked to move only a few miles north, who raised hell: they asked endless questions about everything from the commute to the lighting. They were the usual collection of non-conformists: there was one who rode a unicycle to work and another who preferred a medicine ball to an office chair. But they were also an incredibly strong team – most of them musicians themselves – and the vast and unique codebase they had created was the foundation of the company's success. So quite apart from the human dimension and the blow to morale that would result from mass defections, we had good reason to want to keep them on board. It took a fair bit of persuasion and wrangling, much of it by Alison (who became COO), but in the end almost everyone made the move.

The next obvious question was what to do with the product. I think the Finns had originally been under the impression I would steer the company towards Hollywood in some way, but it had quickly become obvious to me that Sibelius' customers were working musicians and those hoping to become working musicians. The sprinkling of Tinseltown glitter on its shoulders might have persuaded a few customers that using Sibelius would propel them to soundtrack gigs or Grammy nominations, but the big untapped opportunity was in schools, music colleges and universities around the world. So we released a cut-down version of Sibelius for students, together with educational licences, and schools rapidly became an important part of our customer base, via bulk purchases by local education authorities. Eventually Sibelius came to be used by almost 80% of those UK schools where music was taught.

As for the professional musicians, Sibelius already had a dominant position in the UK, but there was scope to grow elsewhere. Our other key market was Australia, where we had a distributor based in Adelaide. That distributor sold other products, too, but Sibelius accounted for about 40% of its business, and as our profitability increased and our confidence grew, we started to build up a 'war chest' for possible acquisitions. We received word that the owner of the Australian distributor might be interested in selling up; after a protracted series of early-morning phone calls we agreed to acquire it and established Sibelius Australia.

The company also had a small sales effort in Walnut Creek, California, led by Philip Nicol (who is now on the board at Dolby Laboratories). With Philip's help we put more resources into the United States in a bid to win a bigger share of the score-writing market there. That meant going head-to-head with Sibelius' only real competitor: a product called Finale, made by the Minneapolis-based firm MakeMusic, which held a similarly commanding position in the United States to the one we enjoyed in the UK and elsewhere. That kind of rivalry plays out slightly oddly: in a duopoly of this kind, any marketing that one company does ends up being promotion for their rival too, as a potential customer will naturally end up comparing products. So we were slugging it out feature by feature. Every time we added new bells and whistles, so did MakeMusic, and vice versa.

Remarkably, there was also a Japanese version of Sibelius which had been developed at considerable expense, but without any distribution agreement in place. After several visits to Japan, we eventually signed a distribution deal with Yamaha – the first time, I believe, that the Japanese company had ever agreed to work that way with a Western partner.

We were aware that there was also a degree of vulnerability in being a single company with just one product. We had developed a narrative about helping technology to enable creativity, while staying out of the way. So we began to explore the potential for related products that would also be useful to our musician customers and which we could distribute and maybe acquire. We also ramped up work on integrations with other applications – since by now even those making traditional-sounding music were using digital editing and production tools, such as sequencers like Cubase or Logic, or the Pro Tools digital audio workstation made by the US firm Digidesign, later acquired by Avid Technology.

All these are deeply familiar components of the software business today. Cheap, bulk educational licensing is the norm, the expectation being that students will continue to use your products once they enter the world of work. Everybody now operates globally because internet commerce and app market-places have made it easy to market and distribute software to customers everywhere and anywhere. And competition today is more between rival ecosystems – Microsoft's Office 365 versus Google's G Suite, say – than it is between individual applica-tions – that is, Word versus Google Docs.

But beyond the nuts and bolts, there was the community spirit we cultivated around Sibelius. Our customers felt a remarkable sense of personal engagement with our products. That was mostly to do with the way in which we made sure that the product was easy to use, an intuitive automation of drudgework which allowed users to be creative without worrying about the chores. But it was also a result of Kerr's brilliant marketing and product positioning. Our end users felt deeply involved in the evolution of the product. We heard their requests and requirements, and responded to them. Product manager Daniel Spreadbury lived and breathed our software: he owned every aspect of it and had personal relationships with many of our key power-users.

All this added up to amazing customer engagement: it's the only product I've been involved with where I would walk into a room, introduce myself and people would say: 'Thank you, thank you. You changed my life. I love your product.' That is quite a moving experience – and quite a daunting responsibility. Get a new feature right and you can earn enormous praise: but make a change that annoys people and there is hell to pay – as Sibelius's later owners would find out to their cost.

Given this strength of feeling, we felt we had almost an obligation to build an online community: it was part of the mantra of the time. We created a browser extension called Scorch, which allowed Sibelius scores to be used online and enabled basic transposition and printing. That allowed the formation of an online community of composers posting their own work, commenting on each other's compositions and selling their work to other musicians.

At its peak, it had a membership of 20,000 or so – an impressive number at a time before Facebook was even founded. We were convinced for some time that the real value of the whole business was in this online capability, but we simply could not create the kind of scale necessary to monetise it. As we'll see later, trying to scale up a niche market profitably turned out to be less effective than getting to scale more or less indiscriminately (and unprofitably), as the likes of Facebook did – *then* slicing and dicing the userbase into countless niche markets and monetising them using a common infrastructure.

So for the time I spent at Sibelius, its core product remained by and large an application that you bought, quite possibly in a shop, which came on discs with an extensive printed manual in a shrink-wrapped cardboard box that you took home and installed on your computer. That box was an important piece of the marketing: we spent hour upon hour deciding how it should look. And how it should work: working out how the manuals, discs and so on would fit into the box took considerable cardboard engineering.

All this expansion was in the service of the Finns' overarching objective: to make it more attractive to a potential purchaser. For a small, shrink-wrapped software company based in the UK to have wholly owned subsidiaries in both the United States and Australia was unusual, but we took the risk and it paid off. Our sales continued to grow, we took on additional staff, we tightened up our management team, and we continued to refine the product.

We were also creating a momentum, and a culture that was ahead of its time. We were able to treat our staff well and respect the fact that so many of them were practising musicians. At one point, we allowed three of them to take a two-month leave of absence to play as a band on a cruise ship. On another occasion, one of our technical team took six months out to work on a Harry Potter film score.

Understanding that a creative company with a creative staff needs to offer a greater degree of flexibility than the norm is becoming more commonplace today – sabbaticals and side hustles abound, and more recently working from home – but at the time we were just being pragmatic. We wanted to hold on to their talent and they wanted to go earn extra having fun playing on a cruise. That idea of work–life balance is something else that has been in danger of getting lost with the rush en route to world domination. One legacy of the Covid-19 pandemic, perhaps, will be to reassert the importance of that balance not just for creatives, but for everyone else too.

Exit, pursued by a bear

{'Crazy', Gnarls Barkley, *St Elsewhere*, 2006}

By 2006 it was clear that from the founders' perspective a sale was back on the table. But for the management team, it was not so clear. We were having a great time, the company was in good shape and business was booming: sales had grown by 20% in each of the three previous years, and we had lots of ideas about how to grow it further. To be sure, there were challenges: the codebase was vast and ageing, and supporting Mac and Windows versions was expensive and complicated. Ideally, we'd have rebuilt from scratch – probably creating a cloud-based solution rather than a shrink-wrapped desktop app – but that was the software equivalent of changing the wheels on a moving car. Overall, though, we could easily have opted to continue developing Sibelius as a standalone business, perhaps taking on an additional round of investment to help things along.

This is a classic source of tension in start-ups: between the founders who saw the opportunity and created a business around it, and the management team brought in to run things, without whom much of its value might never have been real-ised. If these groups differ on the desirability of an exit, there is no obvious resolution. These days, founders will often go to great lengths to maintain voting control of 'their' companies. But if their key employees walk, a lot of the value of the business may leave with them. And with investors in the mix, the picture becomes more complicated still.

As it was, the Finns were the founders and majority share-holders, and thus had both the moral and practical right to make the sale decision, although Sibelius' key investor, the venture capital firm Questor, was technically able to block a sale. But Questor had invested at the height of the dotcom madness in 1999, when valuations were very different to how they looked in 2006. Given that reality, it did not attempt to prevent an acquisition. Our investor director, Simon Acland, played an incredibly supportive role throughout this entire period of the company's development along with Sir Colin Southgate, the chairman. Neither wanted to stand in the way of the founders.

And so an agent was appointed to help make the exit happen. We talked at length with Yamaha, with which we had a good relationship and mutual respect; but the winning bidder turned out to be Avid, with which we had also been working, at arm's length, via its Digidesign subsidiary and the Pro Tools audio workstation. Pro Tools didn't include music notation, so there was an obvious product fit.

The sale was a real moment of triumph for the Finns, whose lifetime of deep engagement with their product had finally crystallised. Even in the closing minutes of the deal, they were crunching through spreadsheets to winkle out its finer details. It was a moment of triumph for me too. I had done the job I had been brought in to do; after the disappointment of Uplister, it was my first big success as an entrepreneur. The team, an incredibly talented and dedicated group of people, would have the backing to take their work to the next level. And ultimately, we were still making a brilliant product that changed its users' lives.

Unfortunately, it didn't stay that way. Avid had a dominant position in digital television, broadcast, and audio editing, but was coming under pressure from Apple. The codebase for almost all its products was long in the tooth, and it had made numerous, wide-ranging acquisitions that had not been particularly well integrated. Not long after the acquisition, Avid went through significant internal changes that made it difficult for the former Sibelius team to maintain our previous, highly productive working practices.

As large companies do when acquiring small ones, it looked to bring us onto its platforms – which meant, for example, trading our nimble accounting package for the corporate system, which was really designed for hardware rather than software. Later, it started to look for efficiency measures, so the Sibelius marketing team was disbanded and its functions folded into Avid's centralised team.

I was no longer the person who had to respond to such challenges: I had moved on to lead Avid's efforts to crack the educational sector. Having successfully developed a community at Sibelius – one that revolved around an online platform where the tools and content could be demonstrated and used – I tried to persuade Avid that the same approach could work there. But the company was not ready to embrace that – the Sibelius community had barely been mentioned during the acquisition process, and certainly wasn't a major component of the valuation.

I learned a lot about the markets for TV and film technology, but grew increasingly frustrated with the way the company focused less on its customers than its share price. So after two years and the expiry of my options earn-out period, I left the company.

Worse was to come. In July 2012, Avid underwent a corporate restructuring, selling off its consumer technology products. Sibelius was retained, but Avid fired Daniel Spreadbury and almost all the brilliant development team, replacing them with an outsourced team based in Kyiv who they thought could do the job of maintaining the codebase just as effectively – and, of course, more cheaply. That was a deeply dubious proposition: Avid was banking on a brand-new set of programmers taking over from a team with decades of experience. 'This is heartbreaking: it took us 15 years to build this business and it took Avid 15 months to wreck it,' said one of the departing devs.

What happened next demonstrated how wrong Avid had been to ignore the Sibelius community. In an unprecedented backlash, concerned users of the product banded together to start a Save Sibelius campaign, with thousands of customers calling for reassurance that Sibelius would not become an 'orphan product'. The suspicion was that Avid would continue to hoover up Sibelius' healthy profits to shore up its financial situation, while the product would gradually decay and ultimately be discontinued.

The campaign ran in large part on social media, notably Facebook, and attracted considerable attention – initially from the music press, but later from the mainstream media too. The Finns let it be known that they had twice offered to buy Sibelius back. Although they had cashed out their financial investment in the company, their emotional investment was still very much alive. But they were rebuffed: the optics for Avid, with its shareholders in mind, would not have been good.

Avid tried but failed to calm the storm; by the autumn, the campaigners were calling on the company to sell Sibelius if it wasn't willing to support it properly. But Avid wouldn't sell Sibelius: as the Finns speculated, it probably couldn't afford to. Its declining financial position led to a shake-up of its management and a rethink of its priorities. Eventually one of the remaining original Sibelius team was put back in charge of its development. The campaigners were pacified – although on their website they reserved the right to rise up again if they felt Avid started reneging on its responsibilities – and they still do.

Cardboard to cloud

{'Muy Tranquilo', Gramatik, *SB3*, 2010}

When the Finns set up their company, it was still quite possible for whizz-kids to use their home computer to write programs that could be sold as commercial products – more usually games than tools. Like most such companies, as time went by it elaborated features and functions, adding to its code and porting to new platforms and operating systems. Over time, Sibelius' commercial success came to rest not only on its millions of lines of proprietary code, but also on its 20,000-strong online community and on the lorry-loads of cardboard boxes distributed to customers around the planet.

Even when Avid bought Sibelius in 2006, it was clear these foundational elements needed re-examining. People were no longer buying software in boxes from shops: they would buy it online for postal delivery, or would just download an installer and the manuals directly. It was becoming clear that applications that could be accessed through a web browser were the future – getting rid of the need to make software that worked across the vast range of Wintel and Apple desktops, a perpetual headache and overhead expense during the early days of personal computing. Cardboard was giving way to the cloud.

Cloud-based software would also be easier to maintain and upgrade. The monolithic codebase that Sibelius had built up over fifteen years was full of complex interdependencies so a change anywhere had knock-on effects all over the place. That meant any new feature required lengthy testing and bug-fixing. The new way of writing applications was to make it modular, using libraries (often open-sourced) and collaboration platforms like GitHub.

In an ideal world, it would have been best to start from scratch, building a cloud-based product on a more manageable codebase. But that is a major project, particularly for a relatively small business. You have to make sure the existing product remains attractive and keep the revenues coming in, while spending heavily on an essentially new product that won't begin to recoup your investment for months, or more likely years. And then there is the major risk that your customers won't migrate with you.

Had the Finns wanted to stay the course, it is possible that the management team would have sought to raise an additional round of investment to finance such a project. As it was, they chose to sell – and Avid, at least initially, chose to ignore the problems of an ageing codebase (which was an issue across many of its products). Instead Avid adopted a classic corporate approach that was all about taking out more and more cost, without regard for the consequent inevitable shortening of the product's lifespan. That left Sibelius as something of a zombie product, lurching along without direction – until the Save Sibelius campaign kicked off.

That campaign was itself a sign of things to come, in both good ways and bad. Today, we are familiar with people mobilising online to protest business or social developments of which they disapprove – encompassing everything from campaigns to save TV shows to the #MeToo and #Black-LivesMatter movements. But to make their voices heard, they typically use a few gigantic platforms – Facebook and its Instagram and WhatsApp subsidiaries, Twitter and more recently TikTok – and mobilise around hashtags or in private groups. What is now much less common is for the community to engage directly with a business. A business will just make use of social media to attract attention. That's not in itself a bad thing, but as we will see in the next few chapters, the fact that communities and their associated data are owned by a few titanic companies means that much of the potential evident in the early web has never been realised – to the frustration of creators and founders and perhaps to the detriment of their fans and customers. For me, companies becoming disenfranchised from their own customers was one of the major negatives of the dotcom era.

When we built a vibrant online community around Scorch, we could see that it had the potential to be a massively valuable extension of the Sibelius franchise to a potentially huge global audience – the digital iteration of the worldwide distribution network we had built up for the cardboard-box product. What it needed was scale and, to achieve that, it needed investment. Unfortunately, Avid at that time was simply not interested and a valuable opportunity was lost. By the time it had changed course, the company had lost a lot of valuable expertise and goodwill, and 'online community' was beginning to mean something very different.

Fortunately, not everybody failed to see which way the wind was blowing. The development team that Sibelius had worked so hard to assemble and retain stayed together after they were given their marching orders by Avid. Just a few months after their departure, Daniel Spreadbury announced that they had moved en masse to Steinberg, a subsidiary of Yamaha. There, they started to build a new musical notation system, Dorico, taking all the learnings (but none of the intellectual property) from their experience on Sibelius. This time, there would be no cardboard involved at all: it would be wholly based in the cloud. The product had completely dematerialised: it was a digital world now.

4

POWER TO THE PEOPLE

{'This Is the 21st Century', Marillion, *Anoraknophobia*, 2001}

While I was at Sibelius, helping to make a great tool for composers, things had been going from bad to worse for the record labels. With the tech companies interested only in the utilitarian deployment of music to drive clicks and flog gadgets, it became obvious that artists – for so long treated as mere serfs by the record companies – were becoming central to the ways in which money could continue to be made in the music industry.[1]

The artists had, for better or for worse, mostly been left out of the shenanigans of the dotcom era. The labels felt no obligation to share any of the money they extracted from start-ups, and since most acts' contracts made no mention of digital spin-offs, there was little compulsion for them to do so. For that reason, they also avoided innovation that might empower artists – for example, the ability to gather precise playback data, allowing them to understand exactly when and where specific tracks were being played, and by whom.

This data has considerable marketing value, but the labels preferred an ostrich-like strategy of deliberate ignorance: if they didn't have that information, they couldn't report it to the artists, and the artists wouldn't have any leverage to ask for more money. The exception was a handful of superstars whose commercial and legal clout allowed them to dictate their own terms, but these weren't normally included in any dotcom deal anyway – an extreme example being that the Beatles didn't appear on iTunes until 2010.

This might have seemed a canny tactic at the time, but the labels were sacrificing long-term strategic benefit for short-term financial gain. Capturing data and using it to build a relationship with listeners was one of the key advantages of digital over physical, and one that has been exploited to prodigious effect by streaming titans like Spotify and Netflix – effectively cutting the labels and other intermediaries out of the loop. My own company Semetric offered to share this sort of information with labels and studio, as we'll see in Chapter 6, but was snapped up by Apple to power its own services.

Even if they were cut out of the dotcom largesse, some artists nonetheless found ways to build productive relationships with their fans – just as we had envisaged in the days of The Raft. In 1997, the quirky UK rock band Marillion was unable to afford a North American tour to promote its ninth studio album, as keyboardist Mark Kelly explained on the online mailing list. What happened next took the band by surprise: the fans got together and collectively raised the funds needed for the tour to go ahead.

Two years later, the band were at the end of their recording contract and unimpressed with the new deals on offer. Rather than getting day jobs, as their manager suggested, they fired him and asked their fans to advance them the recording costs for a new album. It took two days for 6,000 backers to sign up – and the world's first crowdfunded album, *Anoraknophobia*, was duly released in 2001, with distribution through EMI. The crowdfunders got a special edition with bonus tracks and lavish packaging.

Artists have always raised money from family and friends

to buy equipment, book gigs and make demos, but this was the first time a band had used the audience essentially to bypass the industry. It came as something of a shock: here was proof of concept that even the most unstarry of acts could go it alone. But Marillion was an unusual act: major label backing had made the band big enough to attract a dedicated fanbase, whom they had cultivated because mainstream tastemakers had little time for them. At that time, not many bands had that kind of intense online following, and there were no established platforms or mechanisms for crowdfunding. So not many acts even tried to follow Marillion's lead – at least, not for a decade or two.

Back to reality

{'15 Step', Radiohead, *In Rainbows*, 2007}

For artists effectively cut out of digital, one response was to double down on physical. Seeing an artist live was the opposite of the sterility of buying their music online: the visceral, communal and ephemeral nature of a gig still had greater social resonance than downloading a single at your desk.

Playing live promised to let artists grow their audiences, particularly as large-scale festivals – sanitised versions of 1980s raves, travelling rock roadshows and Glastonbury clones – began to proliferate. Despite clichés about screen-obsessed 'digital natives', millennials turned out, like their parents, to sleep under canvas, revive the banjo as a lead instrument, eat organic food bought from inorganic vans and indulge in mood-altering substances with both friends and strangers. Mintel reported that between 2005 and 2010, sales of tickets to music festivals increased by nearly 70%.

With luck and hustle, an up-and-coming band could end up playing to huge crowds, albeit often crowds waiting more or less patiently for the headliners to turn up. This was generally lucrative only for established artists. Because digital distribution made it trivial to keep back catalogues available, 'legacy artists' didn't even need to release anything new to sell huge numbers of tickets and T-shirts. For younger bands it was about building a fanbase – but it could be an expensive way to win over listeners.

For that reason, many turned back to the digital world. What had been a device of convenience for the determinedly untrendy Marillion became standard operating procedure for a new generation of artists: in particular MySpace, launched in 2003, gave artists a convenient place to showcase their work and communicate with fans. It generated its fair share of success stories: during the noughties, 'internet sensation' became part of the hype around emerging artists. But there were a *lot* of internet sensations. That made it hard for wannabes to stand out online. And of course, listening to music posted on MySpace was free.

So despite these new ways to win over listeners and build a fanbase, it still wasn't easy for new acts to make a living in the post-digital musical landscape – unless, that is, they used their internet celebrity or live performance skills to pave the way to a record deal. And if they did, then it was back to business as usual. Real talent is still a rare and fantastic thing, but plenty of people have enough chutzpah to take a stab at it. So there are always more artists wanting a record contract than there are contracts on offer. This does not make for a strong negotiating position. It led to take-it-or-leave-it offers, following an A&R (artists and repertoire) strategy sometimes unkindly referred to as 'there's always another shmuck around the corner'.

Impecunious bands, desperate for their big break, remained eager to sign contracts written by record company lawyers, complete with clauses making expensive provision for things like breakages and packaging, which hadn't been relevant since vinyl's heyday. In exchange, they might get a hefty cash advance, which mostly would never earn out, while the labels took the key rights to their music and to any opportunities those rights might bring as the landscape continued to evolve.

On the artists' side were managers, who supposedly represented their interests in exchange for 15–20% of their earnings. But the quick way for them to make a buck was (and is) to sign a deal with a big advance, and move on to the next opportunity, rather than getting bogged down in campaigning, marketing and touring – still less exploring new and untested avenues. As the history of popular music amply demonstrates, there have always been managers happy to exploit, rather than represent, new talent.

Obviously, managers do have an interest in making their artists successful; after all, their reputations depend on it. But they too benefit from the over-supply of talent. Many of their clients settle for fame even if they grumble privately about the lack of fortune. Only about 10% of signings make good, but managers can talk up their successes while washing their hands of the failures – and are very keen to keep good relations with the labels, who write the cheques for both hits and misses. Only the most powerful managers – those representing the megastars who can name their own terms – are likely to question the system.

Given the dwindling number of physical records to be pressed, and the dwindling number of physical outlets to send them to, successful artists did have some leverage, and new kinds of deal emerged during this period, pioneered by more progressive managers: independent production deals, distribution licences, digital-only deals and '360 deals' which covered any and all revenues associated with the music. With live music on the ascendant, record companies tried to get involved by demanding a share of artists' touring revenues. Such efforts were not well received: the industry got a nasty shock when, in October 2007, Madonna announced a new deal signed not with a record company but with the events promoter Live Nation.

That same month, Radiohead took an important step in trying to break the mould. The band, established as a global brand through over a decade of touring and marketing investment by EMI, and encouraged by a far-sighted management company, engaged with the reality that paying for music was now merely optional. It independently released *In Rainbows*, an album downloadable on a 'pay-what-you-want' basis, as well as in several collectible physical editions. As with Marillion, the band was out of contract and the self-produced album was a distinct departure from its previous work.

It's never been entirely clear how successful Radiohead's gambit was. Despite much talk of a new 'trust-based' economic model, there were clearly vast numbers of people who paid little or no money for the download. But many of them were simply curious and would never have bought it anyway, or so the argument went. Sales of the physical editions, presumably to the Radiohead faithful, were reportedly brisk: the band was said to have made £3m overnight – possibly more than they would have netted from a conventional release. Only the band's accountants knew for sure, and they're not telling.

This obscurity made for easy criticism from both those keen to defend the status quo and those who wanted to destroy it. 'You don't choose how to pay for eggs. Why should it be different for music?' said Lily Allen, who had herself shot to stardom by posting her music to MySpace. Indie veterans Sonic Youth said it was a clever marketing stunt that 'makes everyone else look bad for not offering their music for whatever'. Nine Inch Nails' Trent Reznor, on the other hand, said Radiohead hadn't gone far enough: he launched his *Ghosts I–IV* on an even less restrictive basis the following year.

Others were admiring. 'Radiohead makes business plans the new punk rock' ran a headline in *WIRED*, including testimonials from some of the band's peers. 'They're a genius band, and what they're doing is really interesting,' said Tim Burgess of the Charlatans, which had given away a single at about the same time. But few other bands could afford to make such an expansive gesture as to give away a whole album. One of Radiohead's managers told the magazine that the experiment had been 'a solution for Radiohead, not for the industry'. Fair enough: now the challenge was to find a solution for the industry.

We all stand together

{'Echoes', Pink Floyd, *Meddle*, 1971}

In the face of all this, a group of London's more thoughtful A-list managers began to argue that if only the artists they represented were better organised, they would be better able to control their own destinies. One of the leading lights was Peter Jenner, who in the late 1960s had abandoned a teaching position at the London School of Economics to become Pink Floyd's first manager. He had always taken a politicised view of how artists were treated by the record industry, a stance shared by his current client Billy Bragg.

Jenner got together with a few other A-list managers, including Brian Message, a former EMI colleague of mine who had gone on to work with Radiohead, and Tim Clerk, the pioneering manager of Robbie Williams. The record companies had been pressing for new laws to tackle digital piracy, and the managers saw an opportunity to realign the industry in a way that would get their clients a fairer deal. That, of course, was precisely what the labels didn't want: their biggest fear was having to embark on a wholesale renegotiation of artists' contracts, given the impact of the internet.

The managers had been chewing these issues over for a while at their talking shop, the Music Managers Forum, but recognised that they would have to make a splash if they weren't going to go back to the usual industry haggling. The fundamental changes they were seeking to make to the industry's architecture required a new organisation, one that put the artists themselves in the public eye. And so they decided to set one up.

The Featured Artists Coalition (FAC) was to be all about giving a voice to the performers whose names and pictures adorned records (rather than rank-and-file session musicians, who were already represented by the Musicians' Union). The managers stayed in the background: the organisation was fronted by a board featuring such luminaries as Nick Mason (of Pink Floyd), Dave Rowntree (Blur), Ed O'Brien (Radiohead), Billy Bragg, Sandie Shaw, Howard Jones and Robbie Williams.

At around this time, I was talking to Ian Hargreaves, a media studies academic from Cardiff University who was advising the UK government's Intellectual Property Office on the drafting of the Digital Economy Act. Hargreaves was anxious to understand the perspective of the creative community, so I introduced him to musicians like Mason and O'Brien so he could understand their perspectives. The more we explored the absurdities around intellectual property and the internet, and the anomalies thrown up by applying existing recording contracts to the internet without addressing or changing them, the more I became convinced there was something that needed addressing about the way artists' contracts had been structured or interpreted.

I didn't have much to gain from this personally. Post-Sibelius, I was exploring new entrepreneurial opportunities in music and beyond, some of which are described in the next chapter. But I still believed in the liberating power of the internet and felt that there were some fundamental injustices affecting the rights of creative people. So I helped put the FAC together and eventually, as a relatively neutral figure, agreed to serve as its part-time CEO when it launched in March 2009.

The organisation wanted a seat at the industry negotiating table. It didn't necessarily know what it wanted to negotiate, exactly, but conversations began quickly with the record labels, collecting societies and the live music establishment. The labels' initial welcome quickly grew muted as it became clear that the FAC would be critical of the status quo, and turned into outright hostility as the artists set out to make themselves more politically active.

The UK was in the grip of a general election campaign, with Labour's dour Gordon Brown up against David Cameron and Nick Clegg, both positioning themselves as fresh new faces. In circumstances like these, politicians adored nothing more than to be photographed in a mutual love-fest next to pop celebrities. This chumminess wasn't just about the photo ops, though. The UK's media and technology industries were also in a state of heightened antipathy to government throughout 2009 as debate intensified surrounding the Digital Economy Bill.

The draft legislation contained sweeping measures intended to curtail file-sharing. Despite their unpopularity with consumers, the labels exerted intense political influence, buoyed by common cause with other rights-holders such as TV producers, film studios and book publishers, and the Bill's proposals reflected their most aggressive positioning. Some of the language appeared to have been drafted directly by the British Phonographic Industry (BPI), the trade association for all the major record labels, where I had worked early in my career.

Notable among the Bill's measures were new responsibilities to be imposed on companies that ran broadband networks and provided internet access. These included measures to block consumer access to websites which might be inciting copyright infringement and, most controversially, enforced disconnection from the internet of the most prolific file-sharers. These last had been bestowed with their own term of art, 'egregious offenders', by a highly regarded civil servant who confessed to me that he had been motivated by a desire to 'revivify the English language'. The Egregious Offender sounded very much like a pub I'd want to drink in.

The internet companies wanted none of it. Unlike the music industry, they recognised that policing their customers was unlikely to engender commercial success. Tiscali, a British internet service provider (ISP), had fallen out publicly with the BPI in 2008 after the latter made a peremptory and poorly evidenced attempt to shut down the accounts of fifty-nine of the ISP's customers. The ISPs also pointed out that reliably identifying egregious offenders would not be easy. Proposed identification techniques included scanning of emails, monitoring of internet use and such technical wizardry as 'deep-packet inspection'. With access to the internet now viewed as almost on par with access to electricity or water, the burgeoning digital rights lobby was also outraged, arguing that such measures would compromise privacy, freedom of speech and human rights for no better reason than to protect record-company fat-cat salaries.

The artists found themselves in the middle of this row – and unable collectively to pick a side. Recording artists – and indeed creative types generally – were deeply divided over file-sharing. Some saw it as theft of their intellectual property, with every file shared equating to money being taken out of their pockets. Others saw it as serving exactly the opposite purpose: sharing music with the widest possible audience. And others saw it as simply a fact of life, to be endured or embraced regardless of its morality.

I didn't have a stake in the outcome, but I found it hard to see how the 'crime' of file-sharing could possibly justify cutting off someone's internet access.[2] It wasn't theft in the usual sense of the word – sharing files didn't deny anyone access to anything – and it wasn't clear that file-sharers didn't also buy lots of music. The record companies did have an argument, in the abstract, but that was compromised by their own morally ambiguous behaviour. To my mind – which I expressed gently with my FAC hat on – arguing about whether people should do it or not was beside the point: no one could stop it from happening. I thought we would be better off accepting the inevitable and pushing for ways to increase the value and ease of payment of the official alternatives.

Some high-profile FAC members agreed, giving interviews citing the role that file-sharing played in generating interest in music. 'My generation grew up with the point of view that you pay for your music. Every generation has a different method,' Ed O'Brien was quoted as saying by the *Times* on 10 September. 'File sharing is like a sampler, like taping your mate's music. You go, "I like that, I'll go and buy the album." Or "You know what? I'll go and see them live."' Other luminaries, such as Pink Floyd drummer Nick Mason and Travis singer Fran Healy, made similar points in the same article.

The appearance of that article sent the label chiefs into orbit. They rapidly mobilised the voices of other artists whose opinions were able to be closer to their own. 'I think music piracy is having a dangerous effect on British music, but some really rich and successful artists like Nick Mason from Pink Floyd and Ed O'Brien from Radiohead don't seem to think so,' Lily Allen wrote a few days later on MySpace. That was all very well for giant, well-established acts, she argued, with their 'sell-out arena tours' and 'loads of albums to flog to a new audience' – not to mention 'the biggest Ferrari collections in the world' – but it made it ever harder for new acts to get noticed, sign deals and pay for 'all those pretty videos and posters advertising your album'.

Allen wasn't singing from a totally different hymn sheet to the FAC representatives. In the same blog post, she accused record companies of having been naïve and complacent about technology and argued that 'record company bosses, artists, broadband providers and government should be sitting down' to work out new business models. 'I don't think what's out there is perfect. It's stupid that kids can't buy anything on the internet without credit, forcing them to steal Mum's credit card or download illegally,' she wrote.

In principle, then, there was room for agreement: almost everyone already agreed that file-sharing was inevitable and that better, more consumer-friendly business models were needed. That included the FAC's counterparts in other branches of the music industry, such as the British Academy of Songwriters, Composers and Authors. But agreement on exactly how to balance the costs and benefits was elusive, and Allen's post had transformed an industry discussion into a celebrity feud. The media was quick to jump on board, soliciting the opinions of musicians of all stripes. Battle lines were drawn, with both grizzled veterans and bright young things making it known where they stood, sometimes using heated language.

In some ways, the artist community had been drawn into playing a naïve game against a calculating industry that was carefully positioning its arguments to achieve strategic goals that were well thought through. The record labels had responded with fury to the initial FAC soundings: this peasants' revolt had to be put down before it could get any further. They had already brought to bear the dark arts of 'lobbynomics' and spin and were now mobilising artists willing to speak out against file-sharing. There were whisperings about the extent to which the labels were wielding their control of their acts to make them toe the line in public. A well-known public relations executive was alleged to have written Allen's blog for her.

Whatever the authorship, the effect was to foment a war of words between the artists, but they probably would have ended up at loggerheads even without the behind-the-scenes help. Artists are individualists and mavericks. They may be team players in bands – although that is often a precarious state of affairs – but they are as eccentric as they have to be to make themselves seen and heard. (That goes double for solo artists.) And their commercial circumstances often mean they are competing for attention from both their audiences and their labels.

That makes for artists who are very good at speaking up for what they believe in. And naturally, they have the ear of the media, particularly when they are 'feuding', but that is a double-edged sword. It gets issues aired – without it, the provisions of the Digital Economy Bill might have gone ignored by all but policy wonks and geeks – but contrary to the adage, there is such a thing as bad publicity if you're trying to achieve something more specific than just making a noise. The widening split in the artists' ranks played right into the hands of the labels: it was a classic case of divide and conquer.

Herding creative cats

{'Smile', Lily Allen, *Alright, Still,* 2006}

In an attempt to bridge the divide, the FAC organised an artists-only meeting a week later at AIR Studios, a beautiful recording studio in an enormous old church in Hampstead, north London – owned at the time by the now sadly missed George Martin, producer of the Beatles.

There was an incredible turnout. Members from all sorts of bands showed up including Pink Floyd, Radiohead, Blur, Travis, Keane and Marillion. Solo artists present ranged from veteran singer-songwriter Billy Bragg to soundtrack composer David Arnold and then-hot indie darling Patrick Wolf. Others were on the line: George Michael, working on a new record in an upstairs mastering suite, had a runner providing him with reports of the proceedings; Annie Lennox had her digital representative relaying events by phone.

I had the dubious honour of chairing the meeting. It felt a bit like a cross between a historic parliamentary occasion, an Alcoholics Anonymous meeting and a music industry awards show. It was clearly going to be a rambunctious affair. But any hope I had of running an orderly meeting was rapidly dispelled when, fifteen minutes after the discussion began, an uncharacteristically timid Lily Allen came into the room, clutching a glass of red wine and crouching behind the back row.

Things had not gone smoothly for Allen since she had published her MySpace piece. She had been barraged with criticism and outright abuse from defenders of file-sharing, particularly after the bluntly named website Techdirt had pointed out that her ascent to fame had itself involved her posting online mixtapes which made unauthorised use of other artists' music. In response, she had deleted her blog and announced earlier that same day that she was quitting the music industry.

As Allen was recognised, she was applauded for attending and quickly ushered to a seat in the front. This rapprochement didn't last long, though: the meeting quickly devolved into a live version of the argument that had been playing out in the media. Allen was in equal parts tearful, angry, eloquent and foul-mouthed; her primary opponent in the room was Bragg, ever the 'voice of the people', who delivered a rousing speech about the need to nurture the next generation of fans and man the barricades of protest.

But while half the audience applauded him wildly, the other half scowled, and the arguments swung back and forth for an hour as the debate went on, with artists taking turns to state and restate the positions. Things became increasingly bad-tempered. Musicians glared at each other across the room. Longpigs singer Crispin Hunt got up indignantly, shouting: 'I can't understand why you're being so soft on them. They need to be told what they're doing is wrong,' and marched out of the meeting.

With the clock ticking on and the debate still raging, I felt certain that the room would not reach a consensus on the key issue of disconnecting 'egregious offenders' but maybe could reach a compromise on the positive ideas we all agreed on – respect for the value of music and the need for better models. But as I continued my efforts to draw the meeting to a close, no matter how incomplete, the energy in the room suddenly lifted.

Ed O'Brien from Radiohead suggested that perhaps the answer was not to cut off file-sharers' internet connections, but to restrict their bandwidth. The ability to use email and surf the web would be preserved, but file-sharing would be rendered hugely tedious. The room leapt excitedly on the compromise, the atmosphere becoming euphoric. Bragg stood on a chair and started trying out the precise language of a press release. Or perhaps he was making a proclamation. He and Allen hugged.

There was palpable relief: the community of artists, always shy of confrontation, had found a way to come together. No matter that the proposal would cost more than cutting people off; no matter that people could still file-share, just more slowly; and no matter that 'offenders' would still have to be identified by invasive and unreliable methods.

The AIR Studios meeting ended with a feverish capturing of this compromise, written out by hand on a long scroll of paper by Billy Bragg and Travis lead singer Fran Healy. But by the time it appeared in the press, it was being presented as a qualified backing of the anti-sharing provisions of the Digital Economy Bill. The record companies got their way again – at least for now.

The wisdom of crowds

{'Do It With a Rockstar', Amanda Palmer and the
Grand Theft Orchestra, *Theatre Is Evil*, 2012}

Not long after that meeting, I stood down as CEO of the Featured Artists Coalition. The debate and its resolution had demonstrated that the FAC was capable of assimilating the different views of its members, however scrappily. But to build on that and create a genuine community would require someone who artists regarded as one of their own, and so the board rightly wanted the CEO position to be filled by an artist. The job eventually went to Marillion's Mark Kelly.

As it turned out, the Digital Economy Bill was passed during the dead period between the Brown and Cameron–Clegg administrations; the incoming government had little appetite for its most controversial provisions, and they were never enacted in law. Others turned out to have been redundant, replicating the effect of existing laws. Much of the sound and fury turned out to have been signifying nothing.

Well, not quite nothing. One message that *had* become clear over the course of the decade was 'the band is the brand'. If labels were to stay relevant, they would have to be the invisible hands behind artists' careers, just as advertising agencies guide general consumer brands. Marketing and A&R departments slowly began to accept that they needed to cultivate a new kind of relationship with fans. They would need to understand patterns and trends in musical tastes if they were going to stand any chance of influencing and profiting from them. That pointed to a need for what was increasingly being referred to as 'big data', as we will see in Chapter 9.

Not that this helped artists much. As the decade drew to a close, it was easier than ever for a new artist to gain exposure, but harder than ever for them to earn a living. MySpace lost its way, but Last.fm (founded in 2002), Soundcloud (2007) and Bandcamp (2008) provided alternative forums for artists to interact with fans. Even for those artists who had a record deal, the squeeze that Apple had put on the labels fed down to their acts, while other arenas, such as live shows, had their own difficulties – but new services were continuing to spring up to help artists manage their own brands (as we see in the next chapter).

The idea of going directly to fans for money, as well as exposure, didn't take over the world, but nor did it fizzle out. Marillion and Radiohead drew on their fan communities through one-off web-based interactions. But by the end of the noughties, there were platforms that anyone could use to appeal for funds. Indiegogo and Kickstarter, founded in 2008 and 2009 respectively, allowed creators to advertise projects at a very early stage – no more than a concept in many cases. Both were explicitly aimed at helping creative projects to get off the ground, although they quickly became used to raise funds for everything and anything.

When it works, crowdfunding has the kind of magic touch that the labels lost during the digital revolution. Crowdfunding platforms allow fans a window on a project from its earliest stages onwards, and a mechanism that makes them feel literally and emotionally invested in its success as the project develops.[3] (Social media – following favourite acts on Instagram, say – provides another more immediate means to satisfy the same sort of urge.) The exuberance of videos and the inventiveness of offers that go with each level of donation are key to the excitement around a thriving Kickstarter project: it's not just 'please buy my music', it's about involvement in the creative process itself.

Music fans are cultural consumers who value authenticity and personal interaction alongside a purely material return. Despite the laments written about the poor nature of online consumption, they remain willing to pay for the right product or experience, and that is often better gauged in terms of cultural appeal – which artists are well placed to assess – than according to economics textbook variables like price sensitivity or elasticity. Early on, all kinds of fun suggestions emerged, like giving fans access to a webcam in the studio or in the back of a tour bus. These days, the propositions have evolved into more reliable and predictable offerings. A basic crowdfunding pledge gets you just a copy of an album, while a premium donation gets a special edition or a T-shirt, and larger contributions reap increasingly rarefied rewards, such as lyrical namechecks or access to intimate gigs. The result is that fans often pay far more for a tempting pledge than they would have for a CD and certainly more than for a download.

Of course, it doesn't always work. Many projects simply never get off the ground: even if the work is good, the creator may lack the skills and confidence to make their campaign appealing. And it is easier for those with a little talent and lots of chutzpah to run a successful campaign than the other way round. Others hit their targets but fail to deliver, or are just plain underwhelming – which for fans is particularly disappointing if they've waited months for it to arrive. These platforms have the hustle and bustle of a bazaar, where treasures unimagined await discovery and every price can be negotiated, but the customer can never be too sure of a fair deal or the promised quality.

Perhaps the watershed moment for the crowdfunding platforms was a 2012 Kickstarter appeal by Amanda Palmer, formerly of the Dresden Dolls and spouse of superstar writer Neil Gaiman. Palmer, fresh out of a messy split with her label, asked for $100,000 to make a new album, but ended up raising more than $1m – and then walked straight into controversy when on the accompanying tour she asked musicians to perform with her for 'hugs and beer'. That was a neat illustration of the two worlds that musicians (as well as actors, writers and other creators) now inhabited: those with a measure of fame could turn it into both liberty and fortune, while everyone else gigged eternally in the hope that 'exposure' would eventually convert into hard currency.

A few artists played the long game, patiently building their audiences to give them independence and negotiating power; others had the connections or money to hire good representation off the bat.[4] But more found themselves working multiple jobs, making music in their spare time or around paying jobs. There was little new in that, of course. Aspiring talents have always worked in bars and factories while dreaming of stardom. But this was no longer just the case for hopefuls: it was also becoming the norm for acts with hit songs and significant fanbases to chase one job after another. Digitally displaced musicians were, quite literally, the pioneers of the 'gig economy'.

The facts of the disruption at industry-wide scale were that they produced all kinds of reactions: anxiety and ambition, optimism and fear. The technology models and the business models had all been thrown into the air. It was for the most entrepreneurial to grab the pieces and make something new work. Whether it was musicians or technologists, disruption was provoking everyone and the impact was immense.

5

EMOTIONAL CORPORATIONS

{'Babel', Mumford & Sons, *Babel*, 2012}

Creatives and performers might have been struggling with new ways of taking their art to their supporters, but there was no shortage of companies willing to help. The second half of the noughties saw a new wave of start-ups dedicated to serving creatives in every conceivable respect – developing websites and apps, selling tickets, amassing and interrogating audience data, and developing entirely new experiences like virtual reality.

I was fascinated by this activity but having been around the start-up block a few times, I knew that start-up life was not especially compatible with family life. However, I thought I could still be useful in an advisory capacity to those going through the start-up process.

One such was Mark Meharry, whom I had met in 2007 at a Music Managers' Forum event honouring Peter Jenner, co-founder of the Featured Artists Coalition. Meharry had started a new company called Music Glue that year, as a platform enabling artists to distribute their music directly to fans: its first big release was for perennial digital-pioneering band Marillion, which in 2008 released its fifteenth studio album *Happiness Is the Road* over file-sharing networks. The band didn't approve of unauthorised downloads, but thought it better to reach out to new listeners than ignore or chastise them. So anyone who downloaded the music also got a promotional video message from Marillion inviting them to join its fan community.

Meharry, a New Zealander, had previously looked after technology for the MAMA Group, an events promoter that booked some of the world's biggest acts for some of the UK's leading festivals. Meharry's sound technology background combined with an in-depth understanding of the live music sector gave him a competitive advantage in creating a new kind of disruptive business in this space. In the traditional scheme of things, there are multiple parties involved in making a concert happen. An artist may be represented by an agent, whose job it is to find opportunities for them to play live. These opportunities generally come from a promoter, whose job it is to organise and market the event. That means dealing with the booker at a venue, whose job it is to ensure that the venue hosts events that will earn it a decent return one way or another. And finally there is often a ticket merchant involved, whose job it is to ensure that punters can buy entrance to the gig.

To make matters more complicated still, it's not uncommon for the same person (or organisation) to play several of these roles, and not uncommon for them to do so badly. But they persisted because live music in the noughties was still a world in which personal connections and handshake agreements were the order of business. Outsiders might see this as veering on protectionism. But in some ways, it's also understandable: taking a risk on unproven acts requires trust and relationships that will outlast the occasional washouts and no-shows. But it leaves novice artists exposed to significant risk: even if everyone involved plays with a straight bat – and that is a fairly big 'if' – they can end up making little or nothing out of a gig, or even losing money.

So in an ideal world, acts might seek to dispense with

these intermediaries and find venues and sell tickets directly themselves over the internet. Artists were beginning to buy manufacturing services from labels and license finished records to them, rather than enter into old-school record deals. As far back as 2000, Mark Geiger had started a new kind of online agency in LA called Artists Direct, which started out as an online retailer and eventually sought to break the mould on the live side of the equation. Meharry saw no reason that a similar process couldn't be brought to bear on the live music industry in the UK. He set out to build a self-service ticketing platform that bands could use rather than needing a promoter.

Music Glue aimed to help them do that, as an independent ticketing application, but Meharry's vision went further. If he was working for artists, why not provide them with an easy-to-use platform that allowed them to sell tickets, music, merchandise and other assets in any bundle they chose? This was a more radical idea than it might seem. Because of the origins of the music business, the labels handled recorded music, and event promoters handled live shows: the twain rarely met and were mutually suspicious when they did. And so the platforms that had emerged tended to come from one side or another: Live Nation and TicketMaster on the live side; iTunes and the rest on the recorded side.

Overcoming that divide, particularly as an unknown quantity, required considerable charm, ambition and tenacity on Meharry's part. His role was to become a trusted partner to a bunch of people whose professional careers had been built on never trusting anybody. That was his real talent – that, and a measure of crusading zeal. He felt deeply that the value chain was open to digitisation and disruption – a word which at that time was viewed mostly positively, rather than with the suspicion it often arouses today – and this would be to the benefit of artists. It also made commercial sense: there were new, potentially large customers for his direct-to-consumer platform. Legacy artists, beholden to no label and big enough to secure their own venues, could go it alone. And festivals, which had no permanent infrastructure at all, might benefit from working with a one-stop shop rather than countless middlemen.

Meharry had gone far and wide in search of funds to set up his new venture. His first outside investor was John Matto, a children's clothing manufacturer from Wolverhampton, whom Meharry had somehow persuaded to get involved in the entertainment industry. From day one, Matto took an active interest in the business and was convinced it would bring him a small fortune: he seemed to turn up to every board meeting in a different Porsche. But he has remained consistently supportive of Mark's running of the business.

Meharry had also put a good team together, including some industry heavy hitters: for example, he signed Martin Elbourne, chief booker for the Glastonbury Festival, as an adviser to the company – a man who seemingly knew every band in the world, and who every band in the world wanted to know. Meharry asked me to serve as chair for similar reasons: my music industry knowledge, profile and network were useful assets in developing the business.

It was my first experience as a chair, and it was an open question as to what my relationship with the founders should look like and feel like. To start with there were two of them running the company – Meharry and his techie co-founder – and when the latter decided he wanted to move on after a couple of years, I had to intervene to ensure that a somewhat acrimonious separation was managed without damage to the business. Meharry had already brought someone else into the business, known to everyone as Squadron Leader Joe Porn (his real name is Sri Lankan and hard to pronounce). Joe was influential in the artist community, having among other things shared a flat with Marcus Mumford and Laura Marling and gave the company a lot of credibility early on.

But it was always Meharry who ran the show – both the tech team and the sales and marketing side – and I became something of a coach and occasional fixer for him. Like most start-ups sailing into uncharted waters, it began with a culture of informality, craziness and improvisation. My job was to try to keep things on an even keel and to make sure that they gradually introduced more professional processes of good governance.

The company started picking up clients – a few bands for merchandise, smaller ones for ticketing – but its big break came when it signed the folk-rock band Mumford & Sons as it ascended to global stardom. Music Glue, handling all the band's UK ticketing and merchandise, rode on the coat-tails of the band's success. Mark was interested in bringing in more finance, so I started to help build the strategic narrative and the kinds of financial forecasts needed to attract new investors.

The Mumford & Sons connection was to open an interesting door too. The lead guitarist, Winston Marshall, is the son of Sir Paul Marshall, co-founder and chairman of one of Europe's biggest hedge fund groups. Meharry paid him a visit one day to ask his advice about how to meet the funding gap he was facing, and Marshall senior decided on the spot to invest in Music Glue. Initially Marshall was a relaxed shareholder: it was a significant sum for Music Glue but a relatively small sum for him, and he had many other commercial and political interests to look after.

His presence did make managing shareholders a lot more interesting – it is not easy to balance the expectations of a major hedge fund owner and a maverick clothes manufacturer from Wolverhampton. Music Glue was an attractive business for someone who liked the behind-the-scenes wheeler-dealing – which is to say, it was a great business for Meharry. It was also a good business for some of its early stakeholders, offering a touch of showbiz glamour in the form of occasional tickets or backstage passes.

As such, Meharry had initially taken a rather freewheeling approach to running the company. But the arrival of new, more hard-nosed investment meant the company had to introduce some degree of formality to its operations – after all, we were now working with other people's money. We had to start providing a decent record of how the business was growing: minutes of meetings had to be prepared and approved, and management accounts generated. Board meetings shifted from The Vine pub in London's Highgate Road to the company's offices.

Such transparency was important because investment in Music Glue, like many early-stage companies, was something of a white-knuckle ride. It had a complicated business model and had a few scary brushes with early technology failures. Unlike many early-stage companies, however, cashflow was not a big problem. One of the quirks of the live music industry is that revenue from ticket sales is held in escrow until the gig takes place, because if it is cancelled the money needs to be returned to the fans. After a gig is finished the income is divided up among the various parties in line with whatever agreements have been struck. That means the ticketing platform is sitting on large quantities of cash. The problem, of course, is that without strong accounting it could become unclear how much of that cash actually belongs to it. Add in revenues from merchandise and music, and the picture gets more complex still.

To address this, Meharry had hired an excellent finance

director who eventually wrestled the accounting to the ground and provided a good transparent view of the status on a monthly basis. But even so, the investors still found it hard to understand what (if any) progress the business was making. They consistently demanded more reporting and greater clarity on the narrative. Meharry worked on this together with his version of events, plotting a strategic direction forward for the business, but profits remained elusive, mostly because volume was not high enough, margins were low and the costs of developing the platform remained high.

After a few years, Marshall decided the time had come to shake things up, and moved from being a passive investor to an active board member. He felt that the company should be enjoying astronomic growth, not lurching from peak to trough to slightly higher peak; he made comparisons with Bandcamp, Crowd Surge, SoundCloud, Songkick and Shazam and demanded to know why Music Glue wasn't seeing revenues shoot through the roof. Eventually, he summoned me to several meetings where he asked me what my opinion was and then gave me his view, forcefully. He reminded me of the chair's responsibility to investors, and demanded to know how I was going to make good on them.

My answer was that I would continue both to support and challenge the CEO. I felt that Meharry was still really motivated by his pioneering zeal: he wanted to ensure that the disruption he forecast did actually happen. And although he certainly wanted to make money from it, he wasn't necessarily about to accept a plan from a third party, even as prestigious an investor as Marshall, over his own dyed-in-the-wool knowledge of the industry and how to change it. He wanted to prove his point.

I came under increasing pressure, as the de facto conduit

of investor sentiment, to push Meharry to change strategy or even to step aside. It was a classic City investor tactic: a change of management team could sort out an 'ailing' business. The problem from my point of view was that there was plenty of evidence that this was a risky course of action. You side-line a founder, often the person who knows and cares most about keeping the business running, at your peril. In the case of Music Glue, the founder's many personal relationships were critical to getting deals done in the suspicious world of live music pro-motion. There are many examples from the dotcom bubble of investors unseating founders and putting in their own appoint-ments, normally to dismal effect.

But Marshall also had a valid concern. When Meharry started the business, he had been the fresh pair of eyes looking sceptically at the live events value chain and seeing profitable opportunities to reconfigure it. But it was possible that he had settled comfortably into his role, with its great job satisfaction and relaxed lifestyle, and had 'gone native', unable or unwilling to acknowledge the potential for rapid revenue growth that was apparently obvious from the more detached, less well-informed perspective of his investors.

Be that as it may, in the tug-of-war between Marshall and Meharry, something had to give. As it turned out, that some-thing was me. It made no sense to see Meharry turfed out of his own business, and I suspected expectations that it would soar up, up and away with someone else in charge were mistaken. So I regretfully stepped down as chair, feeling a degree of concern that Meharry would be left to handle the energetic challenges being put to him, but I suspected he would have the resilience to stand up to it too. I had just been introduced to an opportunity to work on a larger canvas and so it wasn't difficult to make the change and run with that instead – but more of that later.

Meanwhile, Music Glue began signing merchandising accounts with some big, global bands, including Iron Maiden, Metallica, George Ezra and Bob Dylan. The scale of the operations needed to support these bands was transformative, nearly doubling the turnover of the company in a couple of years. It has been great to see the business continuing to define a unique place for itself and to grow more than ten years after it was founded. The Covid crisis was punishing for events-based businesses, but Music Glue thrived by being diversified and able to fall back on an appetite for merchandise: in fact, 2020 was Music Glue's biggest ever year. Even Mr Marshall would have to express some satisfaction at that.

Do it yourself

{'Half Life', Imogen Heap, *Ellipse*, 2009}

A few years into my tenure at Music Glue, I came across another platform that aimed to connect artists directly to fans – but that was intriguingly different in its approach both to investors and customers. Juliana Meyer, herself a musician, had founded SupaPass as a platform which let users subscribe to their favoured acts – paying a recurring fee for access to everything a performer or band released, rather than buying downloads, tickets or merchandise on a transactional basis. Whereas Meharry had built a platform that could be used on a one-off basis, Meyer's platform monetised the enduring relationship between artists and fans.

Unlike Meharry, Meyer had not gone after a big-ticket investor but instead raised funds in a focused way from groups of angel investors, many of them following their hearts as well as their heads. 'I always like to invest in companies that are solving problems in society and doing the right things,' wrote one member of a 2018 syndicate. 'I love the idea that Supa-Pass is like a responsible Spotify, which allows artists to share their content with their dedicated fans and retain more of the revenue,' wrote another.

Meyer is the queen of pitching to angel investors; her ability to wow them with the passion, sincerity and ambition of her vision is inspirational. Her ability to convey her story with a force of personality and a convincing financial narrative is a combination that resonates particularly strongly with angel investors. That sense of excitement and continuing growth carries an audience with her and has an underlying strength to it which gives them confidence.

Like Music Glue, SupaPass did not have an easy ride, and when I agreed to become chair in 2015, I found they had some issues in common. Meyer wasn't the subject of the same kind of investor activism as Meharry, but having such a large number of shareholders and a correspondingly complicated capitalisa-tion table brought its own challenges: we had to work out a way of representing shareholders' interests without endlessly cap-turing and responding to myriad individual demands. There was also some catching up to do in terms of the technology that powered the service. Other founders might have decided that riding out the bumps was not for them, or that their company was simply not growing fast enough. But Meyer has a resilience and tenacity that defy scepticism and inspire her supporters to stick with her.

It became clear that the SupaPass service was of interest beyond musicians alone and that it might face less competi-tion in other sectors that had not attracted such a frenzy of innovation. The platform's strength was that it allowed anyone with intellectual property rights to create their own Spotify- or

Netflix-type subscription service, as long as all they wanted to do is make their own content available to their own fanbase. At time of writing, that includes business coaches, fitness instructors, a hypnotherapist, an arts television station and an advertising archive. SupaPass's offering is now more of a turnkey solution for people who want a paywalled website and app with a low level of overhead fees.

Although that is something of a pivot and may seem a less distinctive proposition than the purely music-focused one that got me involved, the company maintained its own sense of mission and focused in on the user experience and making the proposition as easy to use as possible. Having found a new focus, the business challenge becomes all about execution: get the technology working slickly, make the interface really user friendly. Understanding the company's product–market fit and then redirecting and refining that to meet the needs of a precisely defined audience is a valid strategy that yields long-term success if it is well executed and able to scale, at some stage.

I found a common thread in these businesses, based on what I'd seen and learned in San Francisco. They owned their own tech and they understood the integration of tech development to user experience. At the time there were a lot of companies in the UK, particularly in the creative industries, which considered the technology as a black box to be bolted on to the back of their business model. They outsourced their development to others and failed to grasp the nature of technology's integrated role in any properly digital business – from user experience to the choices of platform or technology stack, to the mode of data management to the kind of search optimisation. All these elements that we first encountered at the beginning of Web 1.0 and that have rapidly evolved and matured as we have sped through Web 2.0 and onto 3.0 (which I'll look at later). I wanted to avoid the many tech-phobic companies like that, which still proliferate in the UK. I wanted to invest in founder teams who own their own technology and then help them humanise the application of the technology in their chosen marketplace.

That is the challenge faced by Twine, which has also been diligently developing its own platform to offer something new in the creative industries. CEO Stuart Logan pitched to me when I was judging the UK entry for the Creative Business Cup, an international contest run out of Denmark for start-ups around the world. His company (which was called Clowdy at that point) didn't win, but it caught my attention because Logan combined strong development and technology capability with a good head for business. He had already run a relatively small but successful ad-serving business and now wanted to start a business making it easier for creative companies to store their data in the cloud.

It was a good idea at the time – good enough that others with far more resources to draw upon were already ahead of the game. Amazon Web Services launched in 2006, the same year incidentally that Spotify was founded. Logan was never going to catch them up, but what he was really interested in was helping make life easier for people doing creative work – musicians, illustrators, photographers and so on – who worked with large files and needed to be able to store and share them. The niche nature of that was interesting to me too, and I liked the fact that he was his own product lead – at that stage, the team was just him and one other programmer. Logan was interested in analysing the user activity data as it came in, looking closely at how people behaved on his platform and testing how different users responded to different features and propositions. And he was trying to do this in Manchester, where the investment environment was and remains substantially less benevolent for start-ups than it is in London – let alone in San Francisco.

So I kept in touch with him, as he developed the business and, in fact, pivoted multiple times trying to find a service he could really work through – and he had a few of us advising him, keen to see what he could do. Eventually he landed on a concept which we could all see could scale. Clowdy became Twine, a three-sided marketplace which brings freelance creative talent into contact with commissioners in brands or agencies, while displaying advertising to both groups. The result works for both creatives and commissioners: the former reach a market that is global and often in a hurry; the latter can get their needs met expediently. Logan and his team maintained a rock-solid grip on the technology platform they have developed, keeping a keen eye on the distinct needs of the two main userbases, and iterating features and functions as customers identify strengths and weaknesses.

Twine's story is one which has become increasingly rare – that of the (nearly) lone entrepreneur plugging away, rather than pitching the world and looking for immediate hockey-stick growth. It also speaks to the true importance of business models. Claiming to have come up with a sophisticated new model was all the rage during the dotcom era, and still holds some sway today, but ultimately there are only a few ways to sell online. Building a product that can attract and hold an audience by evolving with them, learning from what they want and giving it to them. The kind of service that gives its users pleasure by providing features before they knew they wanted them, creating a trust and a loyalty through the quality of the experience. We'll come back to these themes later.

Intuition and investment

{'Mr Jones', Talking Heads, *Naked*, 1988}

Music Glue, SupaPass and Twine have three things in common. The first is that they are companies made in the mould of their tenacious founders, and to a large extent remain so despite the twists and turns in their respective journeys. The second is that for years nobody got rich – at least, not by the standards of Silicon Valley, or even by those of 'Silicon Roundabout', the name given to the area around Old Street which became the hub of the UK start-up scene during the late noughties. And the third was that none of them was in fact based there. Music Glue was based in Highgate, Twine in Manchester and SupaPass in Norwich. Post-Covid, all have become virtual businesses. Whether they will ever revert to office working remains to be seen.

These three companies represent one side in a bigger conflict that became tangible across the start-up ecosystem during the noughties. On this side were the passionate entrepreneurs who saw opportunity where no one else could – often taking a leap of faith in starting a business in the absence of hard evidence about any market for their product or service, and then giving all they had (and more) to get it up and running. The other side was typified by the venture capitalists of Silicon Valley, who increasingly demanded 'hockey-stick' revenue growth from a strategy that would massively disrupt a market, grab a dominant chunk of it amid the turmoil and, of course, 'change the world' in the process. The boardroom strife I had experienced at Music Glue, between the passionate founder and the hard-nosed shareholder, was a microcosm of this broader tussle between intuition and investor-led businesses.

The investor-driven mentality was given form in the UK

by Silicon Roundabout, which was lavished with government support in the hope that it would host a start-up ecosystem capable of spawning globally competitive tech companies. It did indeed become home to a large number of ambitious start-ups, and of course a lot of these were heavily hyped and ultimately disappointing.

There were some spectacular flameouts in the digital music space – companies built on huge amounts of hype, an inexperienced investor pool and in many cases seduced by the glamour and appeal of music and musicians. Spiral Frog, Beyond Oblivion and Boinc: companies whose names alone should perhaps have been indication enough to their investors that more money would be spent on lavish launch parties in Cannes or in Las Vegas than in developing a product.

Nonetheless, London remains a magnet for digital music, and a significant handful of such businesses did go on to attract substantial investment, many inspired by the early success of the first music streaming service to scale: Last.fm. Another company, a more slow burning music success, Shazam, launched in 2002 and was one of the most enduring: it allowed people to identify music from a short sample picked up by a phone's microphone, so you could identify a track being played in a bar or on the television just by waving your phone at the speaker. I met its founders, Chris Barton and Philip Inghelbrecht, in Berkeley, California where they were developing the proposition; it became quickly clear that the UK's mobile market was at that time much more advanced than the US market, and so they moved to London where I helped them set up their fledgling business.

But it was really the advent of the iPhone, five years later, that transformed Shazam's fortunes by making it possible to move seamlessly from track identification to transaction. Even then, it was at least another five years before it became unremarkable behaviour to hold your phone up to a speaker to get the name of a track. By the end of the decade it was the fourth most popular free app on Apple's app store and a decent way to sell music, with about 8% of users buying a track after identifying it; and Shazam had the coveted status of 'unicorn': a company valued at more than a billion dollars before its initial public offering.

That unicorn status is still the shorthand for start-up success and to me it raises many questions. To reach a $1bn valuation is likely to be a successful result for early investors for whom timing is everything when it comes to getting in and getting out at the right moments. But it is now increasingly understood that rapid ascension to unicorn status doesn't provide any real guarantee of enduring success. Although there are some very high-profile examples of unicorns turning into titans – Google and Facebook, most obviously – they tend to burn through huge amounts of cash in their early days. WeWork and Magic Leap offer high-profile examples of how this strategy can go badly wrong: sky-high valuations that came undone when the market belatedly realised that the companies were unable to live up to their early promises. The story of WeWork founder Adam Newman is the subject of a major TV series, which can be seen on Apple TV – it's called *WeCrash*.

Unicorn status is now clearly understood as not always a good thing for founders. It took fourteen years for Shazam to start turning a profit and see its valuation balloon to over $1bn. But a year later, in 2017, it sold itself to Apple for less than half of its peak valuation, by which time the founders' equity had been diluted considerably. They weren't alone: the founders of the successful London-based music start-ups Songkick and SoundCloud fared similarly. Of course some founders simply want to make a fortune as fast as possible with little or no regard for the impact of their plans, but others are looking to keep control over a sustainable business that allows them to do what they love, make a difference in their chosen field, and perhaps ultimately build a decent retirement pot too.

Despite this, the runaway success of Google, Facebook, Amazon and Apple reset all expectations of what a 'successful' business looked like, and the Valley Way has come to dominate technology investment and business development. Its adherents pride themselves on a supposedly unsentimental, ultra-rational approach to investment, and a cast-iron belief that overwhelming victory in the market is an end in itself. There is little space in this kind of vision for any but the narrowest endorsement of creativity or imagination, let alone emotion. Nor was there any purpose beyond making money, despite frequent claims to loftier ambitions. As the HBO comedy series *Silicon Valley* showed in brilliant and often hilarious detail, no one ever actually believed the ubiquitous final slide of a pitch deck: 'I want to achieve a billion-dollar valuation and … make the world a better place'.

What Silicon Valley, in fact as well as fiction, shows up so clearly is that greed is an emotion too: that investors are prone to irrational exuberance (hence the dotcom bubble) and markets are driven by 'animal spirits'. In my view, the purportedly sophisticated analysis and forecasting on which investors and shareholders rely is often a smokescreen, a fiction of objectivity that gives them a way to rationalise decisions they want to make anyway, driven by more basic human motivations. The repeated colossal valuations afforded to companies that have yet to turn a profit, and sometimes have no plausible means of doing so, testifies to that. (Although no one can deny the attraction of a 'land grab': a smart piece of market analysis which shows where things are going and sets out a strategy for getting there ahead of anyone else.)

We have been told for decades now that greed is good, and certainly many of the Valley's more libertarian investors would agree. But the rush to enormous scale, and value, often requires a cavalier approach to intellectual property, employment law, regulations and taxation not to mention the wellbeing of employees – factors that are harder to ignore in some domains than others. The results of this are starting to become apparent, through phenomena like the weaponisation of social media and the misuse of personal consumer data which was revealed so starkly and so embarrassingly for Facebook in the Cambridge Analytica affair. Or the appalling behaviours of the management team at firms like Uber. Uber boasted what it called 'a god view' that allowed the management team to see the location of every driver, and every potential customer; it created special versions of its apps to mislead the authorities; and its founder was forced out after being caught on camera abusing one of his own drivers, among other offences.

A corner may have been turned, however. Politicians and regulators are no longer as dazzled by all things digital as they once were, and the public are not so ready to believe that disruption of the old order automatically leads to a better one. It is debatable whether a company like Uber, with its (initially) toxic workplace culture, lax approach to transport regulations, vampiric effects on public resources and bag of dirty tricks to evade regulation, could get started today. Society has grown suspicious about the extent to which technology companies are really benefiting anyone other than a select few stakeholders.

Social movements like #MeToo and #BlackLivesMatter have perhaps made some investors think again about how the long-term success of their businesses relates to their effects on societal health, and about what constitutes acceptable business culture: is it the locker room or something more inclusive? Of course, for the most part, founders with demonstrable ability and good ideas always had, and still have, a choice between following the long, bumpy scenic route of an intuition-led business, or the seductively quick superhighway to world domination offered by a high-pressure investment route, complete with blitz-scaling, rockstar founder CEOs. As social movements start to have an impact and the post-Cambridge Analytica techlash against the GAFA companies (Google, Apple, Facebook and Amazon) steps into higher gear with more imminent EU, US and UK legislation coming to regulate them, it may be that we start to see more founders opting for the former – and perhaps the really smart money will start following them too. But the momentum and successes of companies coming out of Silicon Valley do not suggest that major cultural change has happened there yet.

In their book *System Error*,[1] Reich, Sahami and Weinstein see much of the way out of our current quagmire being led by public investment and the encouragement of governments in liberal democracies to step up to the plate and invest in alternative methods of developing technology responsibly. I'll take more of a look at this further on in Chapter 7 where we'll explore the role of government and public policy to exert and influence on private investment.

On death and dying

{'Gimme Shelter', The Rolling Stones, *Let It Bleed*, 1969}

Let's turn back to the music industry to explore how the emotional impact of technological disruption can affect an incumbent as much as a disruptor. In doing so, I'm picking up on the case of the music industry, though numerous other industries have been wiped out in a similar fashion because of the effects of digitalisation. One of the questions this raises is that, in the midst of constant change and regular disruption, how should companies behave and what might be good behaviour and what might be bad? In the case of the music industry, the reaction to the double-edged sword presented by the combination of the world wide web and mp3 was deeply irrational and distinctly negative. In fact, if you look closely, you can see how it has all the hallmarks of the most profound of all human emotional journeys.

In 1969, Elisabeth Kübler-Ross wrote a book called *On Death and Dying*. In it, she described five stages of grieving which she had identified through many years of working with the bereaved, particularly children. Despite their self-professed ruthlessness and business objectivity, the major record companies' response to the changes forced upon them by the internet closely resembles Kübler-Ross's five stages of grief: denial, anger, bargaining, depression and finally acceptance. I suspect that other sectors have responded in similar ways; certainly the film industry did as much as it could to throw its weight around and try to prevent the advent of streaming services that would profoundly disrupt its only recently established business of selling its films on DVD as well as through cinema exhibitors. The cycles of change are inevitable as technological innovation continues to unfurl with disruptive effects that can be hard to anticipate. So how a company reacts is as important as how it forecasts – and as companies are made up of people, it is human emotions that define companies' behaviour to a much greater degree than traditional businesses have been willing to admit.

Denial in the context of the music industry took the form of ignoring the most innovative and progressive developments, even when they literally came knocking at the door. MP3.com was launched in 1997. The Diamond Rio mp3 player was launched in 1998. All the world's music became available through Napster's free, accessible interface in 1999. Each of these disruptors sought to obtain licences from the major labels. But as I had witnessed at EMI, and experienced at Uplister, such licences were indignantly denied, except on terms so rapacious as to render the supplicants' business models unviable.

Kübler-Ross's second stage of grief is **anger**. In the music industry, anger nearly always takes the form of litigation. In 1998 the Recording Industry Association of America (RIAA) unsuccessfully sued the makers of the Diamond Rio. In 2000, Universal Music Group successfully sued MP3.com for breach of copyright. And in 2000, A&M Records successfully sued Napster for creating an infringing service. Their anger unabated, in 2003, they turned on their own customers under Operation Hubcap, while continuing to lash out with the full force of the law at new file-sharing services like Grokster and LimeWire.

The third stage that Kübler-Ross outlines is **bargaining**. This too was evident. Initially, the labels believed themselves (correctly, if temporarily) to be able effortlessly to extract any gains from the new business opportunities through exploitative licensing deals. But they later shifted to picking up the carcasses of companies they had wrathfully killed off, in the hope that they could be reanimated to do their new owners' bidding. MP3.com was sold to Universal Music Group for $272m in 2001; the following year, Bertelsmann picked up Napster for $85m. Perhaps consumers would accept these zombie services and start paying this time, and get the industry out of the mess it had got itself into? But evidently that was not to be. In near desperation, the industry struck a seminal deal with Apple which it would have cause to repent.

Depression set in as the industry realised that it had ceded its market to invading powers; alienated its supposed customers; watched as its artists were elevated from serfs to barons; and lost its marketing mojo, with its core products being dismantled and commoditised. Unable to persuade anyone that music had value, the record industry watched as it became a mere afterthought to other, more successful cultural products, such as films and TV – and even as other parts of the music industry, notably live performances, enjoyed an exuberant decade of growth and diversification based on higher production values and sky-rocketing ticket prices.

We'll come back to **acceptance** in a moment.

What's curious about all this is how closely these corporate behaviours map onto the very human characteristics that Kübler-Ross so carefully outlined. Companies are 'supposed' to be managed rationally and objectively. Business schools offer MBA courses that preach the doctrine of dispassionate objectivism in business strategy. Businesses are designed with checks and balances to mitigate against the emotional vicissitudes of individual employees. CEOs are respected for their hard-nosed refusal to be distracted from their business objectives by any appeal to sentiment: when the going gets tough, the tough get going. Management objectives are impersonal, with little room for emotion, except of the right variety: positive passion is now allowed (particularly in the start-up sector fuelled by venture capital), but other emotions drawn from the great spectrum of human feelings are rarely acknowledged, let alone welcomed or appreciated.

There are those who would say all this corporate emotion

merely demonstrates the essentially organic, cellular nature of human cultures and societies. The behaviour of individuals is compounded into the behaviour of the whole organisation; the emotion of the individual tessellates into the emotion of the company. While each individual may perform a different task or function, their manners of behaviour and modes of interaction as they relate to each other and to competitors collectively create team culture. The bullish, target-driven objectivism inherent in many business-school approaches has driven the culture of large corporations, in particular, towards brashness and bluntness. And the historic lack of diversity in the boardroom and at senior executive levels has exacerbated that.

Major record labels have always wanted to control everything. That is the mindset. The label is in control: it makes stuff happen even when people don't know it. Record companies were run by people who liked to be pulling the strings behind influential people, events and trends. Whether linked to Live Aid, the World Cup or a general election, major label executives feel they are failing if they are not close to the most fashionable aspect of anything in the national eye. That is part of the excitement – being on the influential inside track of anything hip and happening. As the internet grew in importance, the labels' stance shifted from instinctive denial to bargaining for dominance.

It could also be argued that the labels responded emotionally because theirs is a relatively small and insular industry despite their extensive reach. Its major companies act closely together, frequently, to protect their mutual interests (as, for example, with the 'most favoured nation' clauses written into licensing deals, about which the EU has recently had strong words to say). The group involved in setting the strategic direction for the industry – the ones who got together to launch the Madison Project and the Secure Digital Music Initiative, or approved Operation Hubcap – was so small and close-knit as to provide none of the insulation from emotion that corporations are supposed to build in.

That's not to say that acting emotionally is inherently a weakness. In fact, I would argue that emotional awareness should be a key attribute of any company that deals in creative work. Traditionally, artists have been scouted and developed by the artists and repertoire (A&R) department of a label. The role of A&R staff (much like editors in publishing houses, or dealers in contemporary art) is about building trust with signed artists, and deciding which artists to sign. That was why we used to call them the 'um and ah' department at Virgin. Once signed, A&R has to encourage the artists and point them in commercially fruitful directions as well as being critical and ultimately strong enough to reject work.

That kind of relationship is both very private and very public at the same time. The A&R is the first champion of a piece of music, even before it leaves the studio – and the custodians of whatever secrets or inconvenient truths may be associated with the creation of the work. This implies empathetic and passionate involvement in an artist's or a band's work, and deeply felt engagement in the creative process and its commercial development. That in turn fuels the way the work is presented to the public – the intangible marketing magic the industry seemed to lose sight of during the digital revolution.

Tarzan economics

{'Empire State of Mind (Part II) Broken Down',
Alicia Keyes, *The Element of Freedom*, 2009}

The final stage of Kübler-Ross's grieving process, **acceptance** – coming to terms with the loss and moving on – is perhaps the hardest. As each stage of this emotional journey unfolded, the effects of corporate grief at the passing of a business model became more visible, in both its early denial and its later litigious anger. I have to confess that throughout the noughties, I believed a time would come when the degree of commercial pain would simply be too great for the labels to bear and that radical change would have to come about. I was mistaken – it would eventually come, but it took much, much longer than any of us could have forecast.

The power of current shareholder sentiment should never be underestimated. Investors demand quarterly reports to demonstrate the health of the companies they've bought into. Valuations need to be continually buoyed up by near-term anticipation. Analysts may ascribe some value to long-term strategy, but they will always take more account of the bottom line this quarter. And when push comes to shove, the management team has to accept the wishes of the ultimate owners over their own ambitions for the business.

As I had experienced at Sibelius, it is a big ask to face all this down and embark on the task of building a new high-risk, unproven technology-dependent business, at the same time as sustaining an old-established but dwindling, box-shifting business. It's more likely that the owners of the business will seek to offload it to someone else, who might be willing for their own reasons to make the investment – or to asset-strip it.

Jim Griffin, an advocate for music technology, one time IT

chief at Geffen Records, and owner of the Pho List, a legend-ary newsfeed and chat board for digital music executives, called this challenge of transition to digital 'Tarzan economics'. As companies struggle to find a path through the business jungle, they swing from vine to vine – from business model to business model. To progress, they have to grasp a completely new vine ahead of them while letting go of the one that bore them previ-ously. If the new vine turns out to be weak – the business model unsustainable – it will come away in their hand. If they've already let the old one go, they fall painfully, perhaps fatally, to the ground. But if they *don't* let the old vine go, they won't make any progress – and the old vine will give way eventually.

'We're still clinging to the vine of music as a product. But we're swinging toward the vine of music as a service,' said Griffin in 2008, a time when the record industry was mostly still lashing out angrily with lawsuits. 'We need to get ready to let go and grab the next vine, which is a pool of money and a fair way to split it up, rather than controlling the quantity and destiny of sound recordings.'

Griffin was charged by Warner Music, owner of his label Geffen, with coming up with a way to sell blanket licences to schools and universities – frequent targets of legal action. He devised a platform, Choruss, which would be deployed in various forms at different institutions, allowing a winning model to be identified; it could also be deployed so that internet service providers could collect monies from their customers. But in a painfully apt illustration of the problems of Tarzan economics, Choruss never launched, despite getting several uni-versities and three of the four major labels on board. It proved impossible to enlist or even identify many rights-holders, and the file-sharers whose activity it was intended to legitimise were suspicious. 'I blew it,' admitted Griffin in 2010, before trying to create an international music registry with the World International Property Organisation. That, too, was destined to come to nothing: another vine that couldn't bear the weight.

It is easy, with the benefit of hindsight, to be cynical or even derisive about such efforts. They represented the idealistic side of this period of intense disruption in the industry. The concept of Tarzan economics suggests continuous change, but in many ways the labels were facing a fundamental challenge to the viability of their model.

Spencer Hyman was the COO of Last.fm, before its sale in 2007 to CBS. He phrased the challenge for the music industry very simply. The traditional business model of a music major had three core components, he noted: control the means of manufacture and distribution; control the promotion of music to radio; and control exclusive licensing. The combination of the world wide web and mp3 broke all three.

The resulting void could be occupied by many different models – some of them complementary and others competitive, and with many different associated funding and business models. Very few of these vines looked strong enough to clutch at, particularly from the perspective of an established business still making substantial amounts of money. It's unsurprising that the record companies preferred to find ways to reinforce the vines they were hanging from rather than reach out for new ones. But those vines were fraying – and once the likes of Napster and later Apple and Spotify began sawing away at them, it was only a matter of time before they snapped completely.

6

BY THE NUMBERS

{'Anaconda', Nicki Minaj, *The Pinkprint*, 2014}

While Mark Meharry, Juliana Meyer and Stuart Logan were following their gut instincts, others were taking a more empirical approach. In 2007 while completing his physics degree, Greg Mead was the music editor of *Felix*, the student newspaper of Imperial College London. Keen to stay on top of his beat, he wrote a set of web crawlers to seek out new bands, which he used to ensure that his reviewers were always on top of the next big thing.

The crawler would return data about acts getting written up on blogs and posted on social media. 'I would then go in and see which artists were getting mentioned the most to try to figure out what the cool new music in London was at the time,' Greg recalled in a 2012 interview. 'It worked remarkably well. It really seemed to semi-predict who would be big, and I thought it might be a good idea to commercialise it.'

Not content with disrupting the noble craft of student journalism, Greg decided to build a tool that would collect all the public information about an act showing up on social media in a fragmented way and make it available in a coherent dashboard to the music industry. A computational physicist by training, he knew how to refine the algorithm further; a friend who ran a record label told him the kinds of data they would find interesting. Along with co-founders Jameel Syed, Marie-Alicia Chang and Matt Jeffery, he founded Musicmetric in 2007, with initial funding coming from family friends and angels.

I got involved in 2009, just before the company raised a round of investment from Imperial College's own venture capital arm and Pentech Ventures, a fund based in Edinburgh. I came across the team incubating in the offices of a digital agency that had put a protective arm around them and taken a generous equity interest for their care. The potential was obvious to me, but the team lacked networking contacts in the music industry and were looking for strategic advice. We spent a happy day or two drawing complicated charts of possible markets for our data service. I also met with the early investors and eventually after several weeks of getting to know each of them, they asked me if I would come on to their board as an independent non-executive chair. I was fascinated by the power and potential of aggregating so much data and agreed to join.

Musicmetric's service set out to capture every Facebook like, every Twitter mention, every YouTube play and every Wikipedia page view related to an act. So initially the service was used by artists keen to find out what kind of buzz they were generating, but it was obvious that the data could also be used by record labels, live promoters, marketers or for that matter anyone else with a commercial interest. If you knew that a release was getting traction, you could push it for wider promotion or associate your brand with it in an advert; if you knew a band's last tour had spiked interest in certain cities, you could book them into bigger venues there next time. (Later versions of the system included sentiment analysis, which sought to differentiate between positive and negative commentary – although this turned out to be a much more complex problem to solve and we eventually dropped the feature.)

Separately, and more controversially, the Musicmetric system also tracked BitTorrent downloads. Matt Jeffrey had developed an ingenious way of inhabiting the BitTorrent network with multiple virtual presences that could log into the network and monitor which tracks were being streamed where, and by whom. Given the sensitivity of the labels to this kind of data, it made for some interesting conversations. On the one hand, this was real data, which could be located to individual cities (or even more precisely to IP address), about music that was being actively downloaded by fans, globally. On the other hand, it was an acknowledgement of the scale and precise nature of the piracy problem that the music industry faced. Major labels did not want to do anything that might look like they condoned or in any way saw value in illegal file-sharing activity. So we had to work very carefully around how we presented that data.

But when we combined a view of social media with a global view of BitTorrent downloads, we gained a picture of music consumption and trends in taste that was not visible in any other way. Although labels knew what their own artists were doing, they had no view of how other labels' artists were performing, other than in the good old pop charts.

The charts of course reflected a variety of things, mostly a mixture of radio airplay, streaming volumes and retail sales. That was the one dimension missing from the Musicmetric dataset: sales figures and streaming data. Those mattered because if you could cross-reference online buzz with solid results, you could have much more confidence in your analysis. But the companies that collected that sales information were not interested in licensing it to us on any kind of reasonable terms. Their business model yielded a very good margin and they didn't want to acknowledge the value of alternative kinds of data.

Billboard, for example, would collect data from music stores across the United States, collate it and sell it to record companies and compile it into charts. But when it came to us accessing that information, it was the same old story: Billboard made sure that we couldn't afford it, and no one wanted to partner with us. At best, it didn't see the value of what we were doing; and at worst, it saw us as a threat. It was the classic challenge of a disruptive data play in the middle of an established market. We threatened to offer a more complete, more accurate view – and many of the vested interests would have preferred it if we had just gone away.

We looked for other ways to get the information instead. One early partnership was with Last.fm. The platform was actually the fusion of two separate initiatives. The first was Audioscrobbler, a system for gathering information about what music people were playing on their computers and portable devices. The second was the original Last.fm streaming service which offered playlists – or 'internet radio stations' – based on genre tags or artists. Once Audioscrobbler data was combined with Last FM data, the system could produce more personalised playlists.

The whole thing felt people-powered – the fact that you had to choose to 'scrobble' your listening was crucial – and was much loved by music fans. And because of this, Last.fm turned out to be a very good way to spot up-and-coming talent. Other social platforms, without a specific bent towards music, were fine as places for established acts to connect with legions of fans. But Last.fm was by fans and for fans (at least initially), and so provided a much better leading indicator of emerging acts and trends. Its sale to CBS was heralded as one of the first big exits in the UK digital music start-up scene. But the acquirer, as is so often the case, soon came to feel it had overpaid, reduced investment in the business and laid off staff until the platform became moribund and everyone, including Musicmetric, looked elsewhere for discovery data.

Between BitTorrent and the range of social media platforms whose published application programming interfaces gave us access to their data streams, we were able to dig deep and reveal fascinating insights. In 2012, we released the Digital Music Index report, which provided an unprecedented look at social media activity and at the scale of torrenting activity. We tracked 405 million torrents and found that 3 billion tracks had been downloaded in the first half of the year. We used that to create 'most popular' charts for different cities in the UK, and for twenty countries around the world.

The report duly made headlines – many of them, predictably, playing up how much the music industry had 'lost to piracy' – and neatly illustrated the power of the Musicmetric system to provide both global and granular analysis of listening patterns. Our aim was to create a dashboard that you could look at and ask: Okay, what is the progress of this track, or that artist, or genre? How does this artist compare with this one, or with an aggregated benchmark? What's getting heavy rotation in this city, or on this platform? How does that compare with elsewhere in the country, or for that matter the world? Over time we developed a platform that did just that, in close to real time, for something like a million artists.

The idea was that artists, record companies, brands and marketeers could use the platform to derive market insights, and that did indeed begin to happen. In one case, a European band's album had leaked onto the file-sharing networks before it had even been released – the sort of thing that can be hugely disruptive to promotional plans. But in this case, the band's manager used Musicmetric to demonstrate that there had been huge interest in the United States, which he then used to secure the band a support slot on an A-List stadium tour of North America.

On another occasion in 2012, Nokia wanted to launch a new phone, the Lumia 900, with a performance by an artist that would take over Times Square in New York. Working with our platform Nokia found an act that had been bubbling in the New Jersey area and therefore would guarantee a big crowd to fill the square, but was not yet well known further afield and so wouldn't charge a fortune to perform.

The artist was Nicki Minaj. She went on to become a global superstar.

Supply and demand

{'Pirate Bay', Netsky, 2010}

Despite such success stories, it was difficult to get the music industry as a whole to engage with our service. The record labels were still depressed about the continuing decline of their feudal kingdoms, and data showing them precisely how the rot was setting in did not cheer them up. For example, one of the headline findings from the Digital Music Index was that blocking the Pirate Bay – the torrenting hub that had taken over from Napster as Public Enemy Number One for the entertainment industry – had had precisely no effect on the volume of downloading. None of this made the task of persuading the labels to use our platform any easier – they were too afraid of being seen to offer some kind of endorsement of the value of BitTorrent.

And we needed the labels to come on board. From the start, Greg had a clear view in his mind of what the product was going to look like. But it was hard to figure out whether to create a low-cost web-based offering aimed at broad uptake, or a more high-end bespoke offering. We had set out to make an online platform that could be accessed by anyone. We prided ourselves on how usable, yet powerful, our platform was. Our prices were low and our pricing structure simple. But people didn't know how to use the data, or what to do with it.

This turned out to be a recurring problem for what came to be called 'big data' – you could collect and distil the data, but many people nonetheless struggled to understand what it might do for them. There was a sharp divide between the large number of individual users who didn't think it was worth paying for at all, and the small number of large clients who wanted to have it all – and to have it their way. It was the classic software-as-a-service dilemma: although we wanted to achieve scale, we also needed to secure a foundational client who would pay a significant sum for a proper pilot that would integrate with the data they owned. The major labels were the obvious targets.

The first label to come around was EMI. It had been attempting to create a dashboard that would integrate all its own internal data with other useful external sources. We came to EMI with a product that integrated a whole range of data sources into a coherent and analysable output, but the company was convinced it could build such a thing with its own team. It took some three years to persuade the EMI management team otherwise. First, they tried to do it internally, then they hired a company in San Francisco as an outsource solution. Finally, after persisting in our discussions with them and convincing them that we were not just another start-up that would disappear overnight, they gave us three months to create a pilot.

Naturally we celebrated this success, but when a business is in an early stage, the securing of a significant landmark contract inevitably has to be balanced with the additional burden it places on the team trying to build your core product. We only had one dev team, and client needs had to take priority, so our in-house plans for platform development had to evolve more slowly.

We were in any case overtaken by events. The embattled music industry was consolidating, and EMI was taken over by Universal; amid the post-merger turmoil there was a massive slowdown in activity. We did continue to develop it and eventually worked with the joint EMI–Universal tech team to begin a refinement of the dashboard, but the shifting internal sands of reorganisation and corporate merger slowed things to a glacial rate.

Later, we went on to secure a contract to do an even larger scale full-blown integration with Warner Music, which not only wanted the data but wanted the data integrated into its own analytic systems. Warner's aim was to create systems that could predict commercial success on the basis of patterns in the data, and to generate reports and recommendations for its marketing team that would help improve the effectiveness of its promotional efforts and possibly even its A&R. That meant a great deal of custom work on our part: it was a long way from the simple self-service portal we had built for artists and managers.

This presented us with a different kind of Tarzan economics problem, one common to many software-as-a-service (SaaS) businesses. Like most SaaS start-ups, we had tried to build a platform that would serve as many customers as possible. But our anchor client wanted something different, so we had to try to develop that platform too. In the gung-ho dotcom days of the Valley, the answer would have been to raise lots more investment and expand development capacity without worrying too much about whether the whole thing was breaking even. But in Europe, after the dotcom bust and the financial crash, the mood was more sober and realising revenues took priority.

Not only did we have a demand side problem, but we also had a supply problem. Our job was to tap into the firehose of data being put out by other services, slow it down to a manageable flow that was still representative of the whole, and then clean it up and turn it into information that could be used to generate reliable insights. But we were critically dependent on access to those sources of data.

BitTorrent posed one kind of challenge: there, it was a matter of monitoring what was going on without any central authority or record, and with potentially misleading or mislabelled content. But in the case of social media, there was a central authority, be that Facebook (founded in 2004) or Twitter (2006), which at that time were still vying with each other for supremacy. We were very dependent on the feeds they made available through application programming interfaces (APIs) to allow other services to tap into their data. Initially, these were relatively open, as was considered good practice in the Web 2.0 milieu from which the social media companies emerged. The idea then was that success lay in creating an ecosystem dependent on your core service. And we were small enough that the calls we were making, either directly or through intermediaries, didn't draw too much attention.

But early in 2011, Twitter started to withdraw its support for third-party developers, mostly small firms that had built apps that people preferred, for one reason or other, over the company's own products: offering different interfaces, or additional functionality, for example. TweetDeck, a UK company grown near Silicon Roundabout, was acquired by Twitter in 2011 for

$40m, and continues to exist within Twitter as a power-user interface on the platform. But such moves were insufficient to prevent Twitter feeling the financial pressure of rival platforms, so it seemingly decided to take the power back and enhance its service – including, for a time, an emphasis on integrating music discovery and playback into the main Twitter platform. Eventually the licence for access to the data that we depended on was removed altogether. Without it, we had to find other ways of arriving at our most meaningful insights.

Facebook, which had always held its data more closely, also guarded it more jealously over time. Initially, the company had positioned itself as the custodian of the 'social graph' – the map that showed how people online were linked by relationships, interests and memberships of particular communities. But over time, it became more interested in holding onto all the value associated with the graph in the form of advertising. It became apparent that it was using its vast hoard of data to supercharge its advertising engines – the social equivalent of what Google had done in search – and was no longer prepared to allow third parties access to it in the aggregate.

The value of these hoards of data became more and more evident. Initially, there was some scepticism over value when it came to personalised advertising: the early capabilities of social networks were clumsy and often missed their mark. But as time went by and the sheer volume of data increased to stupendous levels, the ability to identify and target groups by their shared interests was increasingly seen to be of great value.

Facebook could also use the data to build new products and services – and it knew which ones to build (or buy) by looking at patterns in the data, as well as by looking at the kinds of apps its API users were building. And thanks to network effects, once it picked an application it could put more and more distance between itself and would-be competitors with every user and every data point it gathered.

The disparity between the approach taken by Facebook (and to a lesser extent Twitter) and that taken by the likes of MySpace and Last.fm, was striking. The former emphasised the development of interfaces that encouraged users to post and share, regardless of *what* they were posting and sharing. As we've seen, that approach doesn't in any way reward factually sound or socially beneficial content: a relentless pursuit of growth, a lack of emotional or ethical intelligence, particularly as driven by Facebook's CEO Mark Zuckerberg, inevitably led to a loss of moral compass and set the course for episodes like the Cambridge Analytica scandal. These were investor-driven businesses *par excellence*.

MySpace and Last.fm, on the other hand, had built platforms and services dedicated specifically to music fans. MySpace had shot to prominence by putting artists and fans on the same platform, with huge stars posting their music next to teenagers playing in their bedrooms. They allowed users to express themselves – through the design of their pages and the content they posted. This more engaged audience could be prevailed on to make higher-value transactions – gig tickets, for example. These were at least in part intuition-led businesses: MySpace co-founder Tom Anderson was famously the first 'friend' of every single one of its users and a degree of credibility and authenticity was required by music fans if they were to trust a platform to be their community.

During the first few years of this competition, it was far from obvious which approach would win out. For most of the noughties, music provided a killer edge in social networking, just as it had in sales of consumer electronics a decade earlier. Facebook's lack of a music service was considered a grave weakness in its competition with MySpace, with Zuckerberg's company making various unsuccessful attempts to court the music platforms.[1]

But the music platforms had their own problems. They were outgunned financially and struggling to keep up: the obvious answer was to find a wealthy backer. MySpace had been acquired by Rupert Murdoch's News International in 2005; Last.fm in 2007 by Sumner Redstone's CBS – but both had suffered from the transition.[2] Their new owners, keen to monetise their acquisitions, had pushed through ill-advised changes to the culture and functionality that alienated their users – again, something of a repeat of the experience when Avid had acquired Sibelius. And in the unforgiving climate that followed the 2006–08 financial crisis, what marketing money there was went to the social sites instead.

So to the chagrin of those of us who had expended blood, sweat and tears on crafting services that would appeal to the hearts, minds and wallets of customers, it was the first approach that won out: build scale and then find a business model, rather than the other way round. At Sibelius, we had successfully built a community around our product – but it was increasingly the case that communities and discussions were hosted by the big social media platforms, rather than by the companies or brands themselves. Facebook promised to cater to *all* your interests at one location, even if in practice it might not do so particularly well. This 'lowest common denominator' approach helped it to build a userbase so vast that even its most niche subgroups – Facebook users interested in say, Southeast Asian classical music – were also vast.

Over the closing years of the noughties, and into the following decade, the dedicated music platforms lost ground to the generic social media sites. Facebook, in particular, was said to have lured away those interested more in social networking than specifically in music. That might be true, but it could also be the *making* of a music service. When, in 2009, Facebook co-founder Mark Zuckerberg enthusiastically endorsed a new music platform, that was taken as a strong signal that it was one to watch. It was, of course, Spotify.

Data, data, data

{'Happy', Pharrell Williams, *Girl*, 2014}

The appeal was obvious. Spotify co-founder Daniel Ek had succeeded where almost everyone else had failed, by persuading all the major labels, and a key consortium of indies, to license him their entire catalogues. His timing was right, his experience in building Trade Doubler gave him a great track record of growth, and the labels finally realised they needed to back one of the numerous players knocking on their doors – as the shareholder clamour for change grew louder. And they wanted one who would both grant them equity as well as large sums of money – and who looked likely to succeed. Zuckerberg's endorsement was followed by a partnership agreement that saw Spotify more closely integrated with Facebook than any other music service.

A lot of companies had tried, and simply failed, to combine the funding required to develop a platform and license the music, much less find a paying audience. But there had been a few other services with deep enough pockets to sign deals with all the majors – notably Rhapsody, which had evolved out of Listen (a former stablemate of Uplister in the August Capital portfolio, which later went on to acquire the husk of Napster). In many ways, Spotify's success was due to Ek's brilliance and focused determination, but he had great timing.

It was no coincidence that 2009 was the same year that Apple dropped copy-protection from the entire catalogue of songs on iTunes. Streaming looked like an alternative to paid downloads, which were increasingly out of the labels' hands – and this time, the labels insisted on taking a hefty chunk of the challenger's equity. Nonetheless, Spotify's relationship with the majors was still tense. Having been once bitten by Apple, the labels were twice shy about losing what remained of their precarious grip on power.

Unlike Apple, however, Spotify had no separate or supporting business model to speak of (beyond the somewhat tentative nod to advertising) and its rapid growth meant it was paying out large and swiftly mounting sums in licensing fees even as it urgently had to build its subscriber base against the imminent arrival of head-to-head competition in the form of Apple Music. Spotify tried to find ways to differentiate. At the time, it looked as though integrating streaming, social media and live events might be a viable model: Spotify was closely integrated with the Songkick events platform. Spotify's chief economist, Will Page, had recently moved there from PRS for Music, the UK collection society, where he had become quite well known for his work adding up and publishing the total turnover and growth numbers of the UK music industry across all its revenue streams, not just the record business. Page and his team at Spotify worked together with our Musicmetric data science team to see if there was a way to make our various streams of data add up to a fuller narrative: if you were streaming and tweeting about a band, were you also likely to buy a gig ticket?

Our teams continued to work together and in 2013 we did a piece of work that made use of Musicmetric's exclusive BitTorrent data to explore the extent and impact of illegal streams of music data in the Netherlands (where Spotify had just launched) compared with the uptake of streaming services. That work came up with two interesting insights.

The first was that most people torrenting material did so only sporadically. Most file-sharing activity was due to a relatively small hardcore of file-sharers – the notorious 'egregious offenders' – numbering a quarter of a million or so in the Netherlands. The second was that the sharp growth of file-sharing had flattened off at the same time as Spotify's streaming service had become available. We knew much the same was true for iTunes. These results were starting to indicate that legitimate services could pick up the bulk of demand for music, provided they were sufficiently open and their catalogues sufficiently comprehensive.

Daniel Ek had a focus on data for sure, but he had initially been far from clear whether Spotify would turn out to be an advertising platform or a subscription service. His instincts as a product guy were to focus on what the end user needed, and the last thing music fans want to hear is music interrupted by ads. That meant that listeners to ads on his service had to have an incentive to pay for ad-free – i.e. to subscribe. So Spotify decided to concentrate on building up its 'freemium' model, offering paying subscribers a better streaming experience. It continued to build its business based on data, and, in due course, on machine learning intended to make sure that subscribers got exactly the music they wanted, when they wanted it – even if the subscriber themselves didn't actually get to know much about what that music was.

The year after we published our analysis of the Dutch market, Spotify bought the Echo Nest, an interesting business based on the work of two PhD students at the MIT Media Lab. Like the Musicmetric system, the Echo Nest scraped the web for information about songs, but it also analysed the audio content of songs themselves. It 'understood' what music sounded like rather than what was being said about it – thus providing a foundation for everything from recommending songs to listeners to transcribing the parts played by different instruments in a recorded track.

Spotify used the Echo Nest to create 'taste profiles' for every one of its users – a description of their listening habits, grouped into clusters that might or (more likely) might not correspond to recognised genres or scenes. It also built up an idea of the times or contexts in which certain kinds of music might be preferred – while concentrating at work, say, or driving home – with the aim of delivering 'the right listening experience at the right time'. It used that to generate playlists suited to every listener and an enormous range of moods. The showpiece was the algorithmically curated Discover Weekly playlist generated for every user, which astounded many when it made its debut in 2015 with its uncanny ability to suggest music that was unfamiliar and yet appropriate to individual tastes.

It was striking that this was not in principle much different from previous attempts. The combination of Audioscrobbler and Last.fm too had brought together information about individual listening habits and a music library to offer personalised online streaming. But the service was not as slick as Spotify's, beset as it was by licensing issues and doomed by corporate clumsiness after the 2007 sale. Or, to go even further back, it wasn't that much better than Pandora (whose co-founder Tim Westergren I had met while at Uplister), which also ran a streaming service based on music classification. At Uplister, we had recognised that the curated playlist was the logical mode for listening in the post-album era, but we too relied on humans to do the job of curation.

But more to the point, the data, and the ability to make sense of it on the vast scale of 21st-century social networks, simply hadn't existed when we had been trying to put together the pieces of the puzzle a decade earlier. Pandora's Music Genome project relied on humans taking up to half an hour to analyse each song. The Echo Nest, by comparison, did it in thirty seconds. In 1997, the combination of the world wide web and the mp3 had revolutionised how music could be delivered and shared. Two decades later, it was the combination of big data and machine learning that represented the next revolution.

Back at Musicmetric, we built a solid, robust engineering solution: several Hadoop nodes that enabled massive concurrent processing of data. This approach was at the heart of what came to be called the 'big data movement'. But that was only the beginning. We had to hire clever people, who were just starting to be called data scientists, to ask the right questions of the data; we had to spend time exploring the data for anomalies and we had to clean huge amounts of data to make it searchable or analysable at all.

We were trying to assemble and analyse time series of track and artist data and compare them with other patterns of interest and growth, taking into account regional differences and different uses of different social media platforms by fans of different genres in different territories. That, we hoped, would help us understand how songs and artists grew in popularity, who the key influencers were, and how the geography of different groups of fans played out.

Machine learning was making huge strides at this time, but it turned out that the kind of computing power needed to extract such in-depth insights from the data we were harvesting was still far too expensive and inaccessible. Building such complex models and unearthing hidden patterns across such vast data sets required massive amounts of computing and machine learning capability.

We spent a lot of time maintaining our own data on rented server racks at a local data centre, even as cloud-based services were ramping up fast. It was those cloud services that eventually made data-crunching on the scale we had in mind possible: a shift in both scale and complexity that transformed our ability to analyse pretty much everything.

Selling up

{'Uptown Funk', Mark Ronson, *Uptown Special*, 2015}

The music industry might have been reluctant, but music was not the only thing people were tweeting about and download-ing. Once we had closed our additional funding round from Pentech and Imperial Ventures, we changed our name to Semet-ric to indicate an ambition that reached beyond music. We hired a great rep in Los Angeles who started turning up US deals for us and we started to think about the practical steps needed to begin building out into other verticals.

If we could provide this data for brands on music con-sumption, then perhaps we could do the same for television shows, games, downloads and streams, for book titles and for movies. That meant further complexities for the product: we now needed to cover not just artist and song title, but TV show names, actors, directors, channels, etc. And that meant lots more development; the appetite for such capabilities from players including international media producers and major consumer brands was encouraging.

But even as we were starting to explore these intriguing new horizons, a suitor came knocking – no less than Apple, intent on continuing to find people and applications that would improve its new music service and improve its ability to compete with Spotify. Suddenly we moved into acquisition mode, and the shutters instantly came down on negotiations with possible new partners.

Apple has an infamously aggressive approach to negotiation, entirely the opposite of the friendly attitude with which it markets its products. Its UK law firm at the time was Morrison Forster, known in the trade as MoFo. The level of confidentiality that MoFo imposed was, and is, absolute. For that reason, I am obliged to draw a veil over what took place once the initial expression of interest had been made by both sides. Even when the deal was done, we were not allowed to acknowledge that it had happened at all, let alone who the third party might be. Eventually of course, information emerges in the public domain and eagle-eyed journalists spot significant changes in reports to Companies House. No non-disclosure agreement can hide such changes, although they can be heavily disguised.

Suffice to say the outcome of these sudden and intense negotiations was good for the founders, the investors and most of the staff. With one or two exceptions the majority of the Semetric team moved across to work for Apple – some in London and some in Cupertino in Silicon Valley, where many of them remain. The outstanding product skills of Greg Mead and the superb engineering and architectural skills of CTO Jameel Syed are now deployed, happily I hope, in the heart of the Apple machine with all its secretive and world-leading exigencies applied. They were both rock stars, and richly deserved their success.

I didn't go with them. Despite Apple's amazing reputation, its closed culture and the confidentiality it had built around its people didn't appeal. Semetric, like the Echo Nest, simply disappeared from public view. Although it undoubtedly made Apple's offering stronger, you have to wonder what the world might have gained if Semetric had retained its independence. Together with the unhappy outcome of Sibelius' acquisition by Avid, I started to believe that selling businesses at this stage might not be the optimal outcome – certainly when you looked beyond the immediate benefit for those directly involved. If we kept selling off businesses in this way, what would it do for the community, for culture and for the economy in general?

The profound impact of streaming on the music industry's business model continues to evolve. Back in the day, the entire industry was focused on two key sets of data, radio airplay and retail sales, and made strenuous and sometimes shady efforts to influence them. Today, streaming has collapsed those two data sets into one, and created whole new areas of influence. Where music companies used to spend time and effort persuading DJs to play tracks on their radio shows, those efforts are now made (in very different ways) to get key tracks into influential play-lists. Despite having said it would never do this, Spotify recently announced that it was willing to place tracks in its powerful playlists in exchange for payment. Similarly, where the music press used to play an important part in shaping tastes, social media now dominates in paid-for and brand-linked promotions.

The new challenge for music companies is to balance the insights arising from the vast amounts of data that surface from every platform, be it social, streaming or interactive, with the desire to create authentic engagement between fans and their music, such that it might still contain some serendipity and some soul. When to trust the data, and when not to: that is the real question.

Digital medieval

{'Rio Grande', Ikebe Shakedown, *Stone by Stone*, 2014}

Of course, the troubles of the music industry were not much more than collateral damage for the newly emergent technology giants. Selling music at a loss, but music players at a profit, put Apple on a fast track to the world's largest market capitalisation. Others followed similar paths to world domination, although starting from different places: Google with search, Amazon with book sales, Facebook with social networking.

Like a previous generation of internet titans – notably CompuServe and AOL – the shared aim of the GAFA companies was to keep their users within their respective 'walled gardens' for as long as possible. Content – chat, news, music, films – was critical to this mission. Life within these gardens was superficially cheap and convenient, with services offered at no financial cost and built to be as frictionless and functional as possible.

But there was nonetheless a price to be paid. Initially, this took the form of either a free service offered in exchange for personal data (Google and Facebook) or great value and convenience but with locked-down content and devices (Apple and Amazon). Over time, though, the common objective became monopolistic control over their users' data. Understanding what their users wanted – what they were searching for, what they consumed, what they bought – brought the GAFA quartet opportunities to sell them more – whether on their own behalf, or as advertising for others.

Software companies began to sell hardware, and vice versa; and all of them developed content plays: Google with YouTube, Amazon with Prime. The business goal became to harvest as much data as possible, and to lock the customer into their cloud, apps and devices: messaging, mapping, storage, digital assistants, smart homes and more. My music is in the cloud, but soon my medical records may be too, as well as my financial transactions, my patterns of energy consumption, records of visitors to my home and even records of who rang my doorbell and then ran away. Having committed to one or another of these vital services, I am much more likely to migrate more of my services to that platform than to mix and match. It is much more convenient to have a single digital assistant, whether Amazon's Alexa, Apple's Siri or Google's Home, which can put events on my calendar, order my shopping and remind me to pay the gas bill, than it is to switch between apps. It has become increasingly difficult to use multiple GAFA platforms together – and almost impossible to use none.

And so the walls of these digital walled gardens have risen ever higher, expanded to encompass more and more of a customer's needs and wants. As they get higher and higher, it is becoming harder and harder to get out. The walled gardens gradually turned into walled castles, and then into walled cities. Within the walls, the overlords of these domains made their own rules.

Competition between these city-states is often to the short-term benefit of consumers. Life can become seemingly so much more convenient, but there is a long-term price to pay in privacy, choice and perhaps ultimately our political freedom. Not being able to move my music from Apple to Google may be a minor inconvenience: not being able to move my medical records may be a matter of life or death. And we may not have much choice in the matter. In 2016 Google DeepMind did a major deal with the NHS to access individual medical records to train Deep-Mind algorithms in exchange for some low-level digitisation. That agreement was severely criticised for lack of meaningful patient consent, among other issues, but the offer has not gone away and as public spending becomes more constrained around the globe, the pressure to give in to those kinds of one-sided requests increases.

So we feel the GAFA influence over everything from the music we hear to the way we vote. We begin to feel more like subjects than citizens. Scattered around the city-states are the cottage-industry businesses of start-ups and the digital small-holdings of individual creators. Many are subsistence workers; most can't survive without the patronage of the GAFA titans, one way or another. Any that become sufficiently influential to challenge their power are rapidly crushed or made offers they can't refuse. A few client states persist, like Spotify or Netflix, but who knows for how long. Perhaps they will be swallowed up in their turn – or perhaps they will merge to benefit from their own economies of scale as the surge in subscriber growth begins to subside and the inevitable shareholder pressure increases.

And all this is supported by a vast population of serfs who toil to provide the content and connections that keep these digital overlords in business. Instagram influencers or YouTube stars who are heroes to their own communities without conveying any sense of how much they are cogs in a much larger machine. Hopes that the internet would provide a liberating force for workers have faded as it's become clear that the new powers-that-be are no more interested in the wellbeing of workers than those they supplanted. Meet the new boss, same as the old boss. Sometimes they are in fact the same boss: record labels, after a period out in the cold, are the main beneficiaries of streaming revenues, while artists continue to busk it in the gig economy. Welcome to the digital medieval.

7

REINVENTING INNOVATION

{'Christopher Walken on Sunshine', Shawn Lee,
Princess Superstar, *Sing a Song*, 2010}

A group of youngsters decide to form a band, at first rehearsing in a garage, then moving on to releases and gigs financed by friends and family. Eventually a talent-spotter picks them up and gets them signed to a label. Money flows freely, but so does the pressure: most acts will never return the label's investment. But a few will become superstars and transform the cultural landscape.

A group of youngsters decide to form a start-up, at first coding in a basement, then moving on to early efforts financed by friends and family. Eventually a scout picks them up and gets them signed to a venture capitalist (VC). Money flows freely, but so does the pressure: most dotcoms will never return the VC's investment. But a few will become superstars and transform the digital landscape.

Granted, this comparison has its limits, but it does highlight some basic commonalities in the way both the record industry and the tech industry think about risk, talent and growth. Despite the creative and financial resources at its disposal, the music industry was unable to come up with its own solutions to the digital challenge, as we saw in Chapter 2. None of the prime movers in music today – Apple, Spotify or TikTok – originated inside the music industry: they were innovators from computer hardware, online advertising and social media respectively. One part of the explanation is that music industry executives are human and therefore fallible. Another part is that innovation is simply hard, but there is a real link between creativity and entrepreneurialism. As David McWilliams wrote in a fascinating essay about James Joyce in the *FT* (June 10, 2022):

> Artists and entrepreneurs are blessed with similar convictions. Both are innovators. They see possibilities where others see limitations, bringing the previously unimagined into being. Both have skin in the game, living in the theatre of risk, performing on the public stage of jeopardy. Failure can be brutal and success is often a prelude to future disappointment but they are driven ever-forward by self-expression.

The connections between creators, the music industry, investors and entrepreneurs could not be expressed more clearly. And we can take this idea a bit further too. It's worth drawing a distinction here between innovation and invention. Invention is radical and usually singular, but innovation is incremental and often multi-modal. Truly revolutionary inventions are often general-purpose technologies like writing, online communication or artificial intelligence. They create entirely new industries and destroy old ones.

Inventors most often work in academic contexts, or in commercial research labs. The digital world we have explored in this book began, perhaps, with Alan Turing at Bletchley Park, laying out the fundamentals of computer science while working on military cryptography during the Second World War. In 1968, Douglas Engelbart of the Stanford Research Institute gave the 'mother of all demos', in which he exhibited a prototype computer system that included almost all the features of the online world, from the mouse to hypertext. Tim Berners-Lee proposed the world wide web in 1989 as a way for researchers to exchange information at CERN, the fundamental physics research facility. These kinds of privileged locales provide the luxury of space and time to try things out and experiment with them without clearly knowing where the work will lead. Sometimes it takes decades for insights to bear fruit. That is the real value of academic, blue-sky research.

Quite often inventors accidentally stumble on transformational discoveries while looking for something else. SMS text messaging was originally intended as a way for maintenance engineers to communicate with each other, but using the phone to transmit text has led to a world in which we all use 'phones' to communicate all day – and those phones have become general-purpose computers, with voice calls becoming a rarity. Now a new wave of invention is upon us – in machine learning, distributed ledgers (aka blockchains) and robotics. The chances are their eventual effects on society and culture will not be what we might predict today – but they will be significant, nonetheless.

Innovation, on the other hand, is much more incremental in nature. As the word suggests, it is more about doing things that we already do in new ways, rather than something no one has ever done before. That does not diminish its importance. For corporations, for governments, for operators at scale, making an incremental innovation stick is much more realistic than completely overhauling their entire business or operating model. Over time, a succession of such changes, each small in itself, can nonetheless add up to that complete overhaul – and without the disruption fetishised under the Valley Way.

Even incremental innovation is hard. Innovation units inside large corporates may identify the big strategic challenges facing the company: I was a true believer in the radical potential of new media at Virgin and at EMI. But although it is easy to celebrate technological novelty and gain a bit of media hype for it, as happened when we launched The Raft, it is much harder to generate earnest strategic intent among senior managers. More often than not, the C-suite wants bells and whistles, not new business models: the priority is for the company to hit its numbers as smoothly as possible, allowing the execs to pick up their bonuses just as smoothly.

So large and well-established companies tend actively to avoid reinvention, or to pretend that it is not happening and focus on gradual, incremental improvements. Internal initiatives are embraced if they improve existing processes but regarded warily or without outright hostility if they threaten to supplant them. Corporate pronouncements about innovation or continuous improvement are usually carefully nuanced about what they promise to deliver, occasionally to the point of meaninglessness. All too often they can appear to be a kind of corporate virtue-signalling, intended to position the company as forward-thinking in public for the benefit of shareholders and regulators, while privately the business-as-usual train rolls along – until it eventually hits the buffers.

Many start-ups, too, are rooted in comparatively modest innovation, although generations of bright young things hungry for attention and investment have claimed that every minor variation on a theme represents a revolutionary breakthrough that will set the world on its ear. That's evident in pitches that begin with something like 'Uber, but for dogs' and end with something like 'So let's all work together to reduce dogs' carbon emissions – globally.' But the mark they make on the world more often arises from spending investors' money and bending rules than from technological or categorical invention.

This makes sense. For a start-up to gain traction, it needs to adhere to many of the same principle as its customers. Those that offer relatively innocuous, incremental changes may find it easier to win early customers than those that offer more radical solutions. Of course, such innovations achieve comparatively modest valuations and are harder to defend against imitators and competitors. In the business-to-business (B2B) space, success can often mean becoming assimilated into someone else's business as usual – and just improving it a little bit.

Business-to-consumer (B2C) apps can be more radical in their approach – they can get started with 'early adopters', and with a bit of luck and skill can enjoy viral growth, and are perhaps more fertile ground for invention. For that reason, B2C can be more appealing to go-getting entrepreneurs: it might appear to be more dynamic and ambitious than B2B. This is often reflected in the mood swings of VCs too, who can at different times or in different firms swing towards or away from B2C. The dotcom exuberance of the late 1990s saw a proliferation of B2C ventures, accompanied by sky-high valuations and rising private investment. But as the boom turned to bust in early 2000, investors' interest swung away from consumer businesses and back to the more manageable world of B2B. Emotional mood swings or objective responses to market conditions?

So the more daring innovation perhaps is capable of generating larger profits – and probably comes with larger risks attached. That means these profits have in recent decades been accrued by start-ups, funded by investment firms, which have nothing to gain by letting the gravy train roll on smoothly, but everything to gain by derailing it. That lack of regard for the way things 'should' be done has sometimes ended up disrupting broader social norms, from paying for music to online promotion of political campaigns with dubious consequences.

Given all this, from an incumbent's perspective, it might be better to start innovating early and in earnest, before a startup backed by big wallets and fronted by a maverick with little regard for 'the way things have always been done' does it for you. Industrial giant disrupt thyself. Rolls-Royce notably responded to new business management thinking in the 1990s that encouraged manufacturers to move from products to service. In the early noughties, the company moved away from selling the jet engines it so magnificently engineered and began instead to work to a servitised model, selling flying hours rather than engines. This was largely beneficial for the company and solved a number of challenges to its simple sales model. However, the manner in which Rolls-Royce set up the contracts for this service created new challenges when it emerged that the ownership of the flight time data was with the clients, not the company itself, thus limiting the development of further data-centric services.

In the music industry, as we have seen, the *invention* of the world wide web and the mp3 clearly created new opportunities for the music business – something the industry began to understand, even if reluctantly, very early on. But it was Napster's *innovation* – putting those two things together to let people share music – that led to the rapid demise of the music industry's business model.

Absent Napster, incremental change might have been an option for the record labels. But that is the real meaning of disruption. The record companies had just started to accept they might have to change the drive band while the engine was still running; faced with Napster they had to acknowledge the growing need to build an entirely new engine. If it hadn't been Napster, it would probably have been someone else. And most large companies, and certainly most public ones, prefer to avoid such dramatic reinventions. It's quick to pivot a start-up; it's very slow to turn a supertanker.

Is there a way to square this circle? In certain contexts, yes. Companies need not embrace disruptive innovation from the outset, and start-ups need not remain forever beyond the pale to prosper. The key is to ensure that big and small companies find better methods of collaboration to work together in mutually beneficial ways. But that requires thinking again about the ways in which we foster innovation in the first place – whether through private enterprise or public sector strategic initiatives. As I was to learn, private and public sectors pursue innovation for very different reasons and in very different ways. Looking at innovation and digital disruption from a sector-wide perspective or from a government perspective provides a totally different point of view.

Going public

{'Get Free', The Clubcasa Chamber
Orchestra, Sly 5th Ave, 2015}

Except for my earliest job, at the British Library, I had always worked in the private sector: first at the record companies, then at entrepreneurial start-ups. Most such start-ups raise cash, spend it at a furious rate to achieve some measure of success, and then either become defunct or are swiftly acquired rather than persevering with their own growth plans. A key part of the problem for UK start-ups is that the UK market is simply too small to support the emergence of global players, and so many early-stage British companies become increasingly under-capitalised as they mature.

That means promising start-ups have to look elsewhere and

for tech companies that has usually meant the United States. But, despite the UK's strengths in finance and technology, and its still-significant manufacturing and engineering clout, there are very few UK companies acquiring businesses at the rate of the US tech giants – or indeed the Chinese tech giants. They innovate through acquisition. The giants are only too happy to help start-ups by providing data, expertise, access to customers or other services – which have the effect of binding the fledgling company to them – before swallowing them whole. That not only consolidates their talent and technology but also removes a potential source of future competition. So many of the brightest UK start-ups are snapped up by GAFA companies. The vast majority of good software businesses in the UK (and in the United States, it must be said) sell when their turnover ranges between £10m and £20m.

For example, DeepMind was founded by three Londoners in 2010 and rapidly became a world leader in applied machine learning – but was acquired by Google for a reported $500,000 a few years later. DeepMind largely maintained its own identity for some years after its acquisition, but most such acquisitions are simply absorbed into their giant owners. Their teams are dismantled, their products 'sunsetted' and their communities disbanded. Very few UK companies succeed in reaching significant scale before they exit.

I had experience of each of these paths. Uplister had run out of road when its B2C innovation proved too radical for investors in the post-dotcom bust. Sibelius had been partially dismantled by its new US-based owners, until its vociferous community had put a stop to that – but it lost a good part of its mojo along the way. Semetric was swallowed whole by Apple, which put its talent and technologies to good use and dissolved its brand and relationships entirely.

The latter two outcomes would have been regarded as 'good' by most conventional, investor-oriented reckonings. And yet I felt that some potential had been lost along the way. Every time a small company is bought out by a giant one, the possibilities it might have opened up are closed down, redirected towards its new parent's goals. The walls of the digital medieval city-states grow a little higher.

It wasn't clear back then what I could do about this sense of unease, other than to continue encouraging my small stable of companies to pursue their ambitions rather than take a quick way out. But as I mulled my options after Semetric's 2016 sale to Apple, an answer presented itself when I was encouraged to apply for the job of CEO of Digital Catapult.

Digital Catapult was then still quite a new organisation – only a few years old. In 2010, the government had commissioned the veteran technology investor Herman Hauser – one of the co-founders of ARM, the influential British chip design company – to investigate how strong university research output could be commercialised more quickly and effectively. That challenge was not unique to the UK, but it was felt acutely here given the country's long track record of inventing things that had been commercialised successfully elsewhere – a cycle that seemed to be continuing in the start-up era.

Hauser's recommendation was a family of technology innovation centres modelled after the highly successful Fraunhofer Institutes, a network of innovation hubs established to help in the post-war reconstruction of Germany. (It was a Fraunhofer that had come up with the idea of audio compression, and thus to the invention of the mp3 that had so disrupted the music industry in the previous decade.) The idea would be to foster innovation in specific sectors, ranging from biotechnology to satellites to renewable energy. Set up as individual not-for-profit companies, and intended to be agile and business-minded, each of these 'Catapult' centres would encourage applied research and development in their particular sector, and the associated foundation and growth of businesses.

The first to be launched was the High Value Manufacturing Catapult, established in 2011 as an umbrella organisation for seven existing centres, including the National Composites Centre (a department of Bristol University) and the Advanced Manufacturing Research Centre (a department of Sheffield University). It was and remains the only such Catapult to be set up in such a way.

Those that followed were more genuine start-ups: the Cell & Gene Therapy Catapult in Stevenage; the Satellite Applications Catapult established at the Harwell Science and Technology Campus; and the Offshore Renewable Energy Catapult, split across Glasgow and Northumberland. Each had distinct objectives, but all had the same basic operating model. Innovate UK, the UK's government innovation agency, provided a third of their funding, another third was to be raised from collaborative R&D funding, and the other third from commercial income.

The fifth Catapult to be launched, in 2013, was the Connected Digital Economy Catapult, the organisation that I now lead. I didn't know a great deal about it prior to the invitation, and what I had heard was not particularly flattering. The perception was that its activities had become increasingly incoherent and didn't add any value. But a few years previously I had provided some consultancy to the Technology Strategy Board, the body that had been charged with setting up the Catapults. Indeed, I had written a plan for a creative industries' catapult which, when presented to the governing board, was promptly merged with an Information Technology and Communications blueprint because both had the word digital written all over them.

So I was well aware of the Catapult's potential ability to address the disadvantages of the growth-at-all-costs 'Valley Way'.

Back in 2008, I had met Iain Gray, who was then CEO of the Technology Strategy Board (TSB). He was giving a keynote speech in the old Agricultural Hall in Islington, a great, boomy cavernous conference centre. In his speech, Gray described how the TSB would drive opportunities to innovate in industry, using taxpayers' money to generate multiples of value for the economy in smart and innovative ways.

I was intrigued, if sceptical. My only previous experience with publicly funded innovation was a frustrating experience at Sibelius when we won some £60,000 of EU funding to build an app that could identify a tune when you hummed into it – quite a hard problem to solve because not many people could hit the notes accurately enough for automated recognition. But the money came with lots of strings: so many, in fact, that we decided to give it back – only to discover that giving it back took longer than it would have taken to do the project. This foundational experience had not left me with a particularly positive impression of publicly funded research projects.

After the last echoes of Gray's speech had died away around the stained-glass rooftops of the Agri Hall, I buttonholed him and asked him what he was doing for the creative industries. His disarmingly frank answer was: 'Well, hardly anything, to be honest. Why don't you come and have a chat about how you might help us improve on that?'

That neatly turned the tables on me: what *did* the creative industries need from government? It was evident that while there was a clear mode of research and development in many manufacturing-based industries – the development of new cars, or pharmaceuticals, for example – innovation in the creative industries tended to be a hit-and-miss affair left to individual mavericks. Grants funded individual creative works, but rarely the technologies and techniques that underpinned them. After a bit of discussion, I signed up as an adviser to the TSB, with the aim of writing a technology strategy for the creative industries that could act as guide to funding and investment over the next three to five years.

The timing was opportune: while the echoes of the first dotcom boom were still bouncing around policymakers' meeting rooms, the start-up scene was starting to heat up again, and the newly installed Tory–Lib Dem coalition government had a real desire to capitalise on its momentum. This was about the same time that Tech City – the cluster of high-tech start-ups in the Shoreditch area – was starting to receive both public and political attention. And so we embarked on developing a research programme with the goal of addressing the specific needs of creative, media and digital innovation.

We consulted widely and tried to bring together the range of ideas and opinions expressed across companies and universities about what technologies might best drive creative opportunities. I found this a fascinating process: participants included the former civil servants you might expect, but also people drawn from a wide range of academic, industrial and commercial sectors. All of them had come together at the TSB's headquarters in Swindon – a long way from the corridors of power in Whitehall – to decide the best way to spend public money on innovation. I took part in many conversations with some very smart people, and always felt like a fish out of water – but looking around a typical TSB meeting room, I was consoled to see that everyone else seemed to feel that way too.

Disconcerting though this sometimes was, it seemed to work, and the Creative Industries Strategy was duly published in 2009. Given the interests of the period, it contained a lot about the value of data – although it wasn't yet called big data. There was quite a bit about digital and cross-platform production: how digitisation of media meant that games, films and TV could all be produced from the same digital assets and therefore lots of time and money could in theory be saved. It was generally well received and allowed us to formulate programmes of funding within its general tramlines.

The purposes to which those programmes were put were instructive to a public-sector newbie like me. A few years later, then-Chancellor George Osborne wanted to motivate Lucasfilm to make the *Star Wars* sequels in the UK. My TSB colleagues and I were instructed to explore the kinds of funding that might address the needs of Industrial Light and Magic (ILM), Lucasfilm's special effects division.

We duly devised a programme focused on cross-platform media production, and the Chancellor miraculously found £15m to steer in its direction, as well as some generous (and thus rather controversial) tax incentives to dangle before the company. Less than a year later, we all found ourselves at the launch of ILM's London studio, with R2D2 and C3PO among the stars in attendance. Osborne, meanwhile, got a namecheck in the closing credits of *The Force Awakens*. What government wants, I had learned, is what government gets. But what do governments *actually* want?

What governments want

{'Cody', Mogwai, *Government Commissions*
– *BBC Sessions, 1996–2003, 2005*}

The concerns of governments are entirely different from those of entrepreneurs or innovators. A government, of almost any complexion, is primarily concerned with *economic development*: with identifying areas of chronic unemployment or under-employment and figuring out ways to create new jobs and hold on to votes. Increasingly, these days, trying to answer the question of what governments want beyond basic popularity is an arduous and impenetrable task. Governments generally want very simple things – quick easy answers to complicated long-term questions. That means being able to provide reasons for lacklustre improvements in the rate of capital formation and how this might be linked to inequalities in wealth distribution and the poor quality of human capital. Answering those kinds of questions requires a lot of behind-the-scenes research, thought and experiment, which is why governments always like to turn to universities and academics for answers and find it much harder to listen to industry and the practical on-the-ground advice of real companies.

Once, this contradiction might have been dealt with by applying relatively simple carrot-and-stick measures to 'national champions'. That is still the case, to some extent, in some places: in Germany or South Korea, for example, state and federal governments still exercise considerable sway over the corporate sector, which can be directed to take a longer-term view over short-term gain – or, more tactically, to be persuaded with a few quiet words to open a factory in a deprived area here or build a useful piece of infrastructure there. Governments around the world are in competition with each other to offer financial inducements to encourage investment in their preferred sectors or areas. But in general, corporate interests are no longer tied with any loyalty or longevity to national interests. Most sophisticated multinational players maintain keen awareness of global innovation hotspots, and in a digital world they can invest pretty much anywhere with minimal fuss and bother.

And although raw manufacturing capability has its place – as China has demonstrated – outsourcing and virtualisation mean that what's important is research and development. Today, there is scarcely a country or city on the planet that does not talk up its own start-up scene, complete with claims of specific expertise rooted in its history and geography. The UK has much to boast about in that respect: it still, even after Brexit, attracts more venture capital funding than the rest of Europe put together. But any individual country, particularly one with a relatively small domestic market, must work hard to attract foreign investment into its research and development.

So innovation, from a government perspective, is about finding new, exciting, more efficient ways of generating new, better paid jobs, attracting foreign inward investment, creating globally competitive exports and in the process creating businesses that ultimately employ more people and pay more taxes. A considerable part of the feedstock for this innovation comes from academic research, which is also funded in considerable measure by the government. The UK government has therefore had a long-standing commitment to encouraging excellence in academic research on the one hand, and to a much lesser extent fostering R&D and innovation in large-scale traditional industry on the other.

More recently, it has also become more highly attuned to the job creation capabilities of the start-up ecosystem and has developed a set of incentives for entrepreneurs and investors. The R&D tax credit for research carried out by companies and the Enterprise Investment tax relief schemes (EIS and SEIS) for angel investors, most consummately combined by the Cameron/Osborne government, succeeded in effectively attracting entrepreneurs from all across Europe, while both national and local initiatives have aimed to encourage the development of start-up-friendly business zones, most obviously the 'Silicon Roundabout' in Old Street.

But what successive governments have failed to do over the last twenty years is to make connections between the energy and momentum achieved by those start-ups and the productivity needs of traditional industry, which still mostly feeds off the stodgier, less disruptive diet of university-led R&D. The approach to investment in R&D and innovation has typically been high level and top down. Rather than engaging with the merits or capabilities of innovative companies, governments have taken their lead from the research strengths and project ambitions of universities and senior academics, as manifested by research publications.

Over the past decade, the Technology Strategy Board first became a body at arms' length from government and then part of UK Research and Innovation (UKRI), and thus a sibling to the academic research councils. Along the way it rebranded as the less technocratic sounding Innovate UK. But it remains afflicted by the imbalance of power in the landscape. There are *seven* research councils overseeing funding for academic interests, but only one Innovate UK dedicated to research and stimulus in the commercial sector. When it comes to entrepreneurs and investors, Innovate's approach is governed by the concept of 'additionality' required to address market failures, which sees public support as justified only if it fills in where the market cannot – because the activity is not (yet) investable, because the kind of investment that's needed is beyond the private sector's reach, or because it is needed to encourage private investment. That need to encourage private investment has become more central in recent years as it has become clear that the UK is lagging other OECD countries in the proportion of spending on R&D as a percentage of GDP. The average across OECD countries is around 2.5%; the UK currently sits at around 1.7% and aspires to achieve 2.4% in the next three or four years.

Although this recognition of how much catching up the UK needs to do, it has not really changed the way that the machinery of innovation funding works. The entire mechanism of how funding decisions are taken at a project level is still modelled on the academic approach to evaluation. The impact of academic, scientific R&D is found in the publication of a paper. That is the motivation largely for activity in the academic world, where publication is required to achieve academic career development. In the commercial world, obviously impact is looked for in improved efficiency, reduced costs, increased speed to market, reduction in dangerous emissions or improvements in safety, but impact may also take the form of increased capability or an improvement in a company's absorptive capacity – or indeed in the form of increased investment in R&D.

This difficulty in knowing how to engage in useful evaluation of a project proposal in the context of more complex and sometimes less immediately tangible outcomes, has repeatedly presented governments with a problem. Ministers want to see big shiny outcomes from large-scale public investments. Projects in research and development and even in innovation tend to be less tangible increases in capability, understanding, technical know-how. And so Innovate UK has struggled to find a satisfactory and independent means to evaluate the project proposals that it elicits from industry.

It may seem odd to dwell on this problem of evaluation, but it goes to the root of much of what holds public sector funding back from being as effective a tool as it could be in industrial strategy. Innovate UK today continues to focus on the assessment of a proposed project's technical and scientific merits. Its standard grant bid evaluation process includes an element that relates to the exploitation of the outcome and a commercialisation plan, but few if any business evaluation criteria are applied.

An applicant company is required to demonstrate its basic financial integrity and viability, but there is none of the investigation into its skills, track record and real-world capabilities that would be part and parcel of due diligence by a commercial concern. It is a paper process, with projects evaluated anonymously and remotely by independent evaluators with varying degrees of expertise. An applicant might bid for a quarter of a million pounds from the public purse, and bank the money, without anyone ever looking them in the eye and asking: 'Can you actually do what your plan says on paper you will deliver?'

A private investor, by contrast, is typically interested in backing a team and a company. Venture capital backs people first, then their ideas and eventually the product. Without the kind of due diligence such investors apply, it would not be clear if applicants could pull off a project, or how they might use it to build a viable business if they did. That leaves the door open to those whose ideas simply can't get funded any other way – or who have squeezed an innovative-sounding idea out of their existing business plan in a bid to secure some last-ditch funding. It's worth adding that there are now quite a few agencies and consultancies whose business it is to write bids on behalf of companies seeking funding from Innovate UK. This has not been challenged largely because their presence is likely to increase the quality of the application. But however good it makes the paperwork, it obviously does nothing for the quality of the applicant.

This system has its merits, and can claim lots of successes, like Magic Pony Technology, SwiftKey, Babylon Health and SageTech, but it has its problems too. Magic Pony was acquired by Twitter in 2016, SwiftKey was acquired by Micro-soft in the same year; both companies had received significant grant funding from TSB/Innovate UK before receiving mul-timillion pound investments from UK venture funds. For the public sector, there is a good economic development story to tell about companies that start off in a coffee shop and end up with a hundred staff in a hip Shoreditch warehouse. But if the company, and its associated economic activity, simply evapo-rates when its funds run out, or migrates across the Atlantic as a result of an acquisition by a tech giant, the ending is much less of a triumph. Having presided over that outcome twice with Sibelius and Semetric, I am less keen than some to see that as a positive outcome, even if the founders did well, financially speaking.

By contrast, there is a distinct shortage of incentives for established UK companies to build commercial relationships with homegrown start-ups. This is despite the fact that many traditional UK companies are comparatively slow to adopt new technologies – a real problem in the global competitive-ness stakes. But incentivising them to do so is politically tricky. Governments typically hate to be seen as 'picking winners' because failures, costing the public purse as they do, come with yards of bad press attached. So it is politically simpler for public institutions to endorse a free-market approach under which individual companies make their own choices – whether that means disrupting or collaborating with existing industry, or selling out to the United States (or elsewhere). It is perhaps politically convenient that so many such companies are swal-lowed up by the GAFA quartet before they have to prove their value in the cold light of day.

But a stronger and more sophisticated approach would be for Innovate UK to seriously consider and analyse the business models and capabilities of companies applying for funding. Its current approach gives little thought to the real-time nature of the market, or how best to introduce a new product to it. Doing so, rather than 'productising' research regardless of its potential value (or the potential disruption it might cause), would strengthen public support for innovation and make it better targeted. Or perhaps Innovate UK could equip the Catapult network with that ability, to take a more strategic approach to fostering new sectors and de-risking investment.

So I believe we have much work to do in the UK to connect these two strands of activity – encouraging entrepreneurs to back start-ups and encouraging established traditional companies to innovate. Each of these strands is individually positive and constructive, but they are not currently working together. The effective stimulus of start-up and scale-up companies is understood and works well. It is creating a substantial ecosystem with a growing number of founders, some of whom, having exited once, are going round again with the benefit of experience. But this does not translate into advances at the level of leading corporations, and thus fails to deliver large-scale economic impact of the kind that governments tend to look for. And although the government at the time of writing may not be in power as you read this, in this area of public policy there are few differences in approach between the mainstream parties. The only question is around the degree of public investment.

But there are signs that some of the thinking around economic development is changing. For the past two decades, Silicon Valley has been the global model for innovation, as evidenced by its countless imitators around the world. The UK alone has Silicon Roundabout, Silicon Fen in and around Cambridge, Silicon Pier in Brighton, and Silicon Gorge in the Bristol–Cheltenham area. But some of the gloss has come off that model in recent years, as sentiment has grown that the Valley Way has led to socially dubious and even outright detrimental outcomes, and doubts about how much economic benefit these companies create given their extremely low effective tax rates and tendency to funnel money to a handful of individuals. Few if any places have succeeded in replicating its success.

So both companies and governments are seeking other ways to function, a trend that is likely to accelerate given the wake-up calls of the Covid-19 pandemic and more recently the war in Ukraine. Part of this takes the form of a resurgence of nationalism and protectionism – or to give it a more positive spin, the increased interest in development of 'sovereign capability', as governments recognise the strategic importance of certain technologies and take steps to protect them, often by exerting influence over the activities of key companies in their jurisdictions. Much of this policy seems to be derived from the United States and modelled on the Committee on Foreign Investment in the United States (CFIUS). CFIUS is an inter-agency committee authorised to review certain transactions involving foreign investment in the United States and certain real-estate transactions by foreign persons, in order to determine the effect of such transactions on the national security of the United States. In January 2022, the UK's National Security and Investment Act came into force; it enhances existing powers and is described by the government as the 'biggest shake-up of the UK's national security regime for 20 years'.

Much of this has been triggered by large strategic acquisitions. For example, the 2016 sale of UK chip designer ARM to Japan's SoftBank investment group was fiercely criticised by some as a huge loss to the UK's technology sector. Five years later, it was announced that the proposed further sale of

ARM to Nvidia would be subject to review on national security grounds, which led to the eventual abandonement of that deal. Conversely, national security was also cited as a reason for excluding a company from collaborating with UK businesses. Huawei, a Chinese telecoms provider and world leader in 5G infrastructure, has been excluded from all UK commercial telecoms networks and dubbed a 'high risk vendor' – an approach that mirrored that of the United States.

This kind of politically motivated market intervention is not consistently applied by Western governments. The EU continues to work with Huawei and allows it to sell network components into its 5G telecoms infrastructure. That itself perhaps reflects a lack of strategic clarity: sometimes the intervention appears strategic and at other times we have seen more opportunistic interventions such as the £400m investment into OneWeb in 2020. But whether we see an exclusion of technology or an acquisition of a strategic interest in a particular approach, the result can often highlight sovereign technology debt, which in turn can also ironically be an opportunity for innovators. Someone needs to build the 5G technology that Huawei is no longer supplying and equally someone now needs to support the OneWeb infrastructure. That then prompts a need for significant compensatory public investment. So aligning public investment with the need to create certain kinds of sovereign capability could foster particular sectors, but sectors take decades to grow, and governments prefer to think in terms of months, if not weeks or even days.

There is perhaps a degree of schizophrenia in this approach. We allow the Chinese to fund nuclear power stations, but not invest in our telecoms infrastructure. This is just one of the contradictions raised by political turbulence and a retreat from globalism. There are many others. If the Valley Way is not replicable or desirable, how else can you accelerate the emergence of entirely new sectors? Should you create specific regional clusters, facilitate the proliferation of start-up companies around academic institutions, or engender more dynamic technology-centric ecosystems in response to industry demand? How can you create more porous interfaces between academic research and entrepreneurial innovation? And which is more beneficial to society and the economy: a handful of unicorns driving shareholder value or clusters of values-driven businesses increasing social cohesion?

These questions are front and centre today. From a policy perspective many of them are perennials and were already being asked in 2016, when I took up the role of running Digital Catapult. The job seemed as if it might offer the opportunity to put what I had learned in the market into practice, and perhaps even to inject some business-driven urgency and risk appetite into part of the public sector. I realised the reputation of the Catapult was not exactly stellar, but I also knew of the impressive reputations of some of the team. I liked the idea of working on a larger canvas; there was the potential to develop something that could positively affect hundreds of companies, rather than the half dozen I was working with directly.

So I applied for the job, entered the competitive process and after all the appropriate procedures and formalities, I got it. And that was when the real challenge started.

Reloading the catapult

{'Into the Dark', Marc Moulin, *Top Secret*, 2001}

When the Connected Digital Economy Catapult was first conceived, it seemed reasonable to regard 'digital' as a discrete industrial sector, more or less synonymous with the use of data. Big data was hot and the idea of data-sharing – between both businesses and individuals – seemed wide open for innovation, given the UK's research strength in computer science. There was an assumption, given the Valley Way, that opportunity lay in building data-sharing platforms that businesses could aggregate around, and that was a major focus for the Catapult.

This proved mistaken. The challenges of data-sharing were not technical, they were commercial. Think about it. If Business A asks Business B to share its data, Business A might reasonably assume that Business B has spotted an opportunity to make money that it might be able to realise itself. And so no sharing happens until Business A is satisfied that it can't monetise the opportunity alone, by which time it has either expired, or Business C in San Francisco has already gone public with the idea.

On top of this, there already was an Open Data Institute charged with a similar mission, albeit focused on public-sector rather than commercial data. Beyond that, the Catapult's projects had no particular sector or technology focus, and the results were hit-and-miss. It was difficult to sum up coherently what the Catapult was for, what it was doing and what difference it was making.

Aware though I was of these issues, they were rudely brought home to me on my second day in the job, when I was due to meet the CEO of a major German manufacturer. The company is also a significant UK employer, so I was accompanied by several senior government officials, all of whom had a good deal of interest in keeping this company on-side. When I stepped into the lift at quarter to nine, I found myself face to face with a complete stranger who was nonetheless glaring at me, accompanied by two poker-faced assistants who kept their eyes fixed on the ceiling as the lift rose agonisingly slowly to the Catapult's offices on the ninth floor.

I was pretty sure, from the brief I'd been given, that he was one of the most senior of the government officials joining the meeting. As soon as we entered the office he pulled me aside into a conference room, barking at the others to stay outside, and proceeded to inform me in no uncertain terms of his extremely negative view of Digital Catapult. From his perspective, at that stage, the Catapult was contributing nothing to the economy and providing the government a very poor return for its £12m a year investment. Given that I had been in my role for only twenty-four hours at this point, all I could do was smile at his inference that I was somehow responsible for this parlous state of affairs. Certainly, he gave me the clear impression that however concerned the board of the Catapult might have been about its standing, it was insufficiently so. The knives were out, and he was leading the charge.

I had already known that the Catapult needed a change of direction: during the recruitment process the then chairman had sold me on the need for the Catapult to make a minor strategic realignment. It was clear from this charged encounter, however, that what was needed was a complete turnaround. We needed a new strategic narrative quickly, which could be communicated readily to our stakeholders in government and to the Catapult's customers in the commercial world.

I thought back to the challenges of economic development that had motivated our work at the Technology Strategy Board and realised that Digital Catapult could do a lot to demonstrate how the adoption of digital technology could help. The Catapult could take its lead from policymakers to address such questions as: how do we drive improved productivity in industry? How do we help high value job creation? How could that in turn drive regional economic growth? And how does society benefit? Key to this, I felt, was encouraging UK entrepreneurs not only to start businesses – in fact, there were already many incentives to do that – but also to grow them in sustainable and socially productive ways, rather than just inflating them forcefully and then selling them before they burst.

I was also convinced that my experience in the creative industries could be brought to bear on this new challenge: the same kinds of disruption that I had witnessed, and the transformations that had followed, were now being visited on an ever-wider range of industries. The next wave of digital technologies – from artificial intelligence to virtual reality and from 5G data to distributed ledger systems – would pose their own challenges. I knew that my background could help traditional industries better understand the challenges of the digital revolution, and perhaps help some of them to avoid the grisly fates of their predecessors.

It was apparent, though, that we shouldn't try to cover everything, nor could we just pick up projects on an *ad hoc* basis. Either approach would be a recipe for incoherence and strategic failure. We needed focus. So we rapidly surveyed the UK's industrial landscape and identified sectors where the digital dividend was likely to be biggest. Our first choice was clearly the creative industries, as they were both early victims and early adopters of digital disruption. Our second selection was manufacturing, because our analysis suggested that widescale digitalisation of manufacturing systems and processes could massively multiply efficiency, perhaps more than in any other traditional industrial sector. These became our customers – the organisations demanding solutions to their problems and improvements to their products and processes.

The other logical step was to think about the supply side

– the technologies that might usefully be applied to the needs of this customer base, or that might unlock new capabilities or efficiencies for them. It was evident that 'data' alone was not sufficiently precise. So we assembled a set of emerging technologies that we thought combined competitive opportunity for the UK with transformational impact for its businesses: digital infrastructure, such as 5G wireless, the internet of things and sensor networks; immersive technology, including virtual reality, augmented reality and extended reality; distributed ledger technology (essentially, the blockchain); and artificial intelligence and machine learning.

Matching technological supply with business demand was central to our strategy, but the key was making that match early. The UK was well supplied when it came to academic research and development, and had implemented many ways – some might say *too* many – to encourage the formation of start-up businesses, ranging from tax breaks to buzzy new business districts. Where it was less well equipped was when it came to supporting those start-ups to grow into mature businesses, which was why so many burnt out or sold out before they could fulfil their potential – especially to the United States, where the potential investment and customer bases were that much larger.

The more we could encourage the formation and development of early-stage businesses, and the more we could encourage traditional businesses to become early adopters of the resulting technologies, the more we could drive their global competitiveness. Start-ups have the freedom to innovate without corporate baggage, but they need customers to bring scale to that innovation. Established businesses, meanwhile, have the clout to invest in promising technologies and turn them into robust solutions marketable throughout the world.

Early adoption can be risky, but it leads to growth and new

opportunities like no other strategy. That's why it had mostly become the preserve of investors with the stomach for risk, and why successful start-ups enjoyed such explosive growth – but also why others turned out, after the initial excitement had died down, to have created little of enduring value. I felt this was an area where Digital Catapult could do what the market could not, using small amounts of public money to support early adoption by building the kinds of experimental physical and digital spaces the market would never provide, and then running great innovation programmes in and around them.

The innovation landscape

{'Gnossienne', Paolo Fresu, Richard Galliano,
Jan Lundgren, *Mare Nostrum II*, 2016}

That was the strategy that we launched in 2016 and that we have pursued, iterated and continued to evolve since then. In that time, I am glad to say that Digital Catapult has gone from strength to strength. We're still in our ninth-floor offices in Euston, but have more than doubled our staff to a brilliant team of over 200. I can't say we've ever reached what you might call a normal steady state. We faced Brexit, a general election, a government review of efficiency and value for money, being placed in special planning (wrongly), then Covid, a war in Europe and raging stagflation. But facing market headwinds like these is why we need to use public money – carefully and strategically – because applied collaborative research and experimentation build new capabilities that in turn generate innovation, but it is hard and risky to do. When times get tough, industry needs support in areas like these, when the natural instinct in the face of economic headwinds is to retrench. That is what a

Catapult can do: bring the level of risk down and signpost the way forward, building the confidence in private and industrial investors to go where they have previously feared to tread.

So we are active in the development of all our five chosen technologies and working with companies in sectors ranging from telecoms to the food and drink supply chain, from media and entertainment to advanced manufacturing. Over £4bn of private investment has gone into companies that Digital Catapult has supported, and more than 400 early-stage companies a year benefit from its programmes.

But like all the Catapults, Digital Catapult has a unique stance. It is steadfastly agnostic in its approach to both technology and commercialisation; unlike many of the large tech consultancies, Digital Catapult has no allegiances to a particular technology approach or vendor, nor does it pursue any particular business model. For demand-side companies trying to navigate their way through competing vendor offerings, an independent and agnostic organisation that can give them impartial advice and insights is vital. In the fields in which it excels, Digital Catapult is valuable for that reason.

But there is more to the Catapult than that. There is a commitment to responsible deployment of technologies, a belief that digitalisation and decarbonisation are dual goals that reinforce each other; there is a strength of commitment to diversity and inclusivity in our people and our partners that we pursue consistently and rigorously. As an organisation we celebrate an openness and curiosity about the potential of technology to be a force for good in business. We have an ambition for the companies we support and an optimism that, despite dystopic scenarios that so much technology deployment invokes, there is still the potential to do more good than harm and that is what we try to achieve on a daily basis.

Digital Catapult has developed a culture that rejoices in and celebrates the diversity of the people who make up the team. We attract and retain brilliant and idealistic people who want to work somewhere where the values we declare are the ones we live by.

We spent a lot of time together as a management team working out how to articulate our values. We didn't want to come out with a set of corporate clichés that get written on some entrance hall wall but don't inhabit people's approach to their work. The four words we came up with were ambition, curiosity, openness and optimism. We try to take those into all our projects.

For example, our Made Smarter Technology Accelerator really helped speed up innovation for the industry giants that joined in, including BAE Systems, Safran Landing Systems and Northumbrian Water Group. It helped them tap into the skills, creativity and the agility of start-ups in their particular areas of advanced technology and together develop ideas that they simply would not have had alone. These programmes go far beyond basic matchmaking by getting into the detail of the barriers holding back those specific corporates, from smoothing supply chains and reducing environmental impacts to finding the right scaleable solutions.

So there is a unique commitment to building capabilities in deeply technical areas such as software-defined networks or the development of digital twins. We build the facilities that allow us and partners to get practical, hands-on experience of the technology set they are exploring. We will run acceleration programmes but they're not like any other generic programmes, they are based around a test bed or a virtual lab and then supported by mentoring, partnerships and collaboration with people who would otherwise never have met. So it's not just about convening players in the landscape, it's about curating the partnerships and developing a technical and business sandbox in which collaborators can play.

Digital Catapult also has to operate in the broader innovation landscape where we collaborate increasingly with the other Catapults and with our parent body Innovate UK, as well as with its Research Council siblings. In addition, there is a plethora of other institutions with related interests which at times Digital Catapult is asked to differentiate itself from. The list is long and meandering, as are the accretions of institutional creation across years of endeavour in their area: Nesta (formerly the National Endowment for Science, Technology and the Arts), the Open Data Institute, the Ada Lovelace Institute, the Oxford Internet Institute, Tech Nation (founded by the Department for Digital, Culture, Media & Sport to fan the flames of Silicon Roundabout), not to mention various other bodies that have occasional overlapping interests.

Most of these bodies have relatively coherent missions – tied to specific sectors, as the Catapults are, or to areas of research, as the Research Councils are – and there is a reasonable degree of strategic alignment and clarity when taken as a whole. Some features of the landscape don't fit together perfectly – as noted above, I don't believe Innovate UK's underlying mission is necessarily well served by the academic ethos it has shared historically with the Research Council, but that is starting to change under its new CEO, Indro Mukerjee, who is doing much to assert a new identity for Innovate.

Nonetheless, both Innovate UK and the Catapults are commercially minded – and that poses some questions about the use of public funds. At one point I overheard colleagues at Innovate UK telling companies that their motivation in providing grants was to make founders rich and therefore able to contribute more in taxes. That made me uncomfortable, even if it was said tongue in cheek. It suggests that the objective of public funding was to help founders make a lot of money, rather than empowering them to be able to achieve something they really believed in, and ensuring it was to the benefit of society. It felt like a crude attempt to translate the Silicon Valley model into the language of public interest.

This kind of discomfort arises regularly at the interface between public investment and private business. For decades, the prevailing assumption in government has been that the private sector is far better at getting things done: politicians of different political complexions over the years have repeatedly called for the supposed efficiency of the commercial world and in some case the apparent discipline imposed by the free market to be brought to bear on the slow and stolid world of public-sector risk aversity. Deregulation, privatisation and public–private partnership have been the order of the day for the duration of the UK's Conservative/coalition government of the last ten years or so.

However, there are also many politicians and officials who still harbour a degree of suspicion of private entrepreneurship, mistrustful that there can be any motive other than profit – and profit in the form of personal fortunes for a few founders and investors, at that, rather than the kind of broader wealth creation they would like. They have trouble with the notion that private companies could act responsibly and even ethically: that seems at odds with the supposedly rapacious, winner-takes-all nature of the free market. The antics of Silicon Valley's billionaires do nothing to assuage this idea.

Both these positions are now eroding – the free market is clearly not the cure for all socioeconomic ills, and entrepreneurs clearly have a role to play in a thriving society – but what remains is the sense that a business must be macho in its pursuit of the bottom line, or else it is simply not a good business. The idea persists that go-getting, take-no-prisoners, ends-justify-the-means behaviour is synonymous with commercial success. Once again, the Valley Way has a lot to answer for here: think of Uber, a ground-breaking unicorn that pioneered ride-sharing, but whose macho internal culture was nothing short of toxic. And, let's face it, there are quite a few traditional businesses eminently capable of standing as the 'unacceptable faces of capitalism'. Sports Direct anyone?

The logical inference is that any grant funding from the public purse must therefore be accompanied by strict constraints and lots of oversight to ensure good behaviour. Of course there is a real need for public accountability and transparency where possible. But from my experience, the levels of governance imposed on many forms of public investment into companies tend to be excessively bureaucratic because of these fears and rather simplified prejudices. There is a stark contrast between the governance imposed on publicly funded delivery agencies, and the levels of scrutiny involved in reviewing academic research – and it is the latter which receives the majority of public innovation funding.

Digital Catapult supports individual companies and indeed celebrates a success when those companies receive private investment, but the overall motivation is always about developing the sector as a whole, about signposting to other investors that this field of technology application (industrial 5G, for example) is a strategically valuable area of opportunity. But in the end, of course, you do this best by practical example of showing success and how something is done in individual companies. And we do that with the intention that others should copy, compete, and leapfrog what has been achieved. In that way, all boats rise.

In this context, it is perhaps unsurprising that maverick voices occasionally call for public innovation programmes that are free of that kind of bureaucracy. It was more surprising to hear that sentiment coming from the heart of government, until it became clear that the source was that most curious and eccentric of power-hungry advisers: Dominic Cummings.

Despite being unceremoniously ousted from No. 10, Cummings survived long enough to see his brainchild, the Advanced Research and Invention Agency (ARIA), into the world. A key architect of the successful campaign for Britain to leave the EU, Cummings argued that the UK's ability to support ambitious 'moonshots' (high-risk, high-impact projects) were being held back by EU State Aid rules. I agree with those who argue that those rules were always implemented more strictly in the UK than elsewhere in Europe: to that extent, Brexit may not so much free us from European rules as from Britain's own red tape.

Cummings' vision for ARIA is interestingly distinct in its refusal to identify particular industrial sectors or technologies to focus on. Instead, it is intended to identify and invest in moonshots by giving genius mavericks broad licence to pursue their ideas with considerable discretion. In that, it is modelled after the United States' Defense Advanced Research Projects Agency (DARPA), which has had a hand in developing many initially speculative technologies (including the internet itself, which started out as ARPANET).

But because ARIA has finite funding – its budget is puny compared with DARPA's – someone will at some stage have to make some key choices about what to shoot for. The key thing about a moonshot, in my experience, is not whether you get to the moon, but all about the fun you have trying to get there and the spin-out products and ideas that come along the way. ARIA might, if it were smart, try out some new kinds of intervention to encourage by-products. What it will actually do is hard to say: at the time of writing, the establishment of this new agency is still being handled in secrecy by the same technocrats whose appetite for governance its creation is supposed to counter. The appointment of a CEO, sourced from the US DARPA programme, was announced with great fanfare only for the appointee to stand down quietly six weeks later, for personal reasons.

So the jury is still out; it is not clear if this new entrant in the innovation landscape is really necessary. The original DARPA was a product of the aftermath of the Second World War, when there was a need to invest massively and rapidly in restoring the US economy. There was not a sophisticated panoply of innovation organisations across the United States, so DARPA was an early prototype that evolved over time. You might argue that coming out of the economic recession caused by the Covid-19 pandemic and the war in Europe will be an economic equivalent of recovering from the Second World War. But unfortunately at the time of writing the prospect of a lengthy recession seems to be growing not receding. So, at this stage of the 21st century, the challenge is not so much a lack of organisations aimed at delivering innovation into the economy (there are plenty of those) but more about the challenge of orchestrating and funding them adequately to match the economic need – whatever tagline we wish to give it.

In other words, we need a clear long-term strategy. Shaping the innovation landscape takes time – it is more about directing continental drift than about just plonking an entirely new continent into the landscape. Unfortunately, individual ministers (and now, it would seem, special advisers) may enter office with a desire to find something that will have a distinctive impact.

Often, cynically speaking, something that can be claimed as an achievement and help boost them up the greasy pole, or perhaps something they will be remembered for. In my experience, it is rare to find a cabinet minister who is not interested in legacy from day one. If their predecessor had invented an industrial strategy, they feel duty bound to rewrite it as a *modern* industrial strategy, which requires their successor in turn to demand that we stop calling it industrial strategy and start calling it, for example, an *innovation* strategy. And so on and on.

Confused policy leads to confused outcomes. Many of the greatest innovations in Silicon Valley have not been based on novel science. Airbnb, Uber and Facebook scaled relatively straightforward applications of technology. Their innovation was to make something (booking a holiday or cab, sending out an annual newsletter to your friends) slightly easier to do than previously. In the UK, we still say we want to commercialise the excellent basic research which comes out of our brilliant universities. We say we want a thriving, iconoclastic start-up scene, but we also want to protect our mature businesses from disruption. Our strength in creative industries, financial services and technology gives us a competitive edge, and yet promising businesses like Semetric end up crossing the Atlantic rather than stay put.

Many of these statements are not contradictory – or at least, they need not be if our innovation landscape was sufficiently joined up, rather than fractured and lumpy, as it is. The reorganisation of the Research Councils and Innovate UK under UKRI may eventually go some way towards solving this, if between them, they can free themselves of some of their protective layers of bureaucracy.

It is certainly time that these bodies developed a collective strategy for research, development and innovation and told ministers what it was, instead of leaving it to be influenced by short term quixoticisms of successive incumbents of No. 1 Victoria Street (which houses the Department for Business, Energy and Industrial Strategy), who move in and out of the revolving security door faster than you can say 'innovation ecosystem'.

None of this is helpful in terms of achieving longer-term economic development goals – or, really, in helping our garage band of innovators to get started either. Entrepreneurs just want to build good businesses, but in our fast-evolving world, what seems like a good idea today may look more like a bad one tomorrow – and a good idea may not make for a good business. But what is a 'good business' anyway?

8

BUSINESS UNUSUAL

{'Kokoro', Fatoumata Diawara, *Fenfo*
(Something to Say), 2018}

The idea that everyone has a book in them is a commonplace. So, increasingly, is the idea that everyone has a business in them. But as the cynical rebuttal goes, just because you have an idea for a book doesn't mean it would be a *good* book. And just because you have an idea for a business doesn't mean it would be a *good* business. The problem, of course, is that in both cases you will probably have to spend a lot of time and effort before finding out if it is or not.

As I argued earlier, twenty years of dotcom mania have given a highly specific meaning to 'a good business' in the digital realm: one that pursues growth at all costs, jettisoning considerations of collaboration, fairness and ethics. But over the past few years, discontent has set in with this approach: the taxes avoided, the abusive behaviours overlooked, the social and environmental harms enacted and the plutocratic privileges created. Increasingly, there is acknowledgement of the degree to which this is no longer acceptable with the rise of the #MeToo and #Black Lives Matter movement, previously unheeded voices are starting to be heard. The other meaning of 'good', for years dismissed as soft-headed and irrelevant, is starting to reassert itself. A good business needs to be inclusive and responsible as well as profitable. It needs to be driven by values, as well as economics. But as many have found, that is not an easy combination to achieve. And for many of the old school investor community, this shift looks like a set of considerations that they may or may not regard as worth taking into account.

So let's just think about this from the point of view of the entrepreneur and start at the beginning, when someone decides to act on that bright idea in their head. Few first-time entrepreneurs know what they're getting into at the outset, whether for good or bad. Sibelius began life as two teenagers' pocket-money hobby and ended up as a globally successful, category-defining product. Uplister, however, started out with a wealth of talent and a pile of money but ended up with nothing. Accidents of circumstance have a lot to do with how the story turns out. But for simplicity's sake, let's talk about the two main kinds of story that entrepreneurs tell themselves when they start a new business.

One kind of entrepreneur is utterly convinced that they have a big idea that will change the world permanently, and for the better, if only they strive hard enough to get it noticed, funded and adopted. This is the assumption behind the Valley Way, as modelled by the likes of Steve Jobs, Jeff Bezos and Mark Zuckerberg. It is encouraged by breathless media coverage and, unsurprisingly, by investors who are only too happy to see their money working hard for them. Let's call them the sprinters.

The second kind of entrepreneur would like to make something work a little differently, a little more efficiently and a little more profitably. As I argued earlier, this is the kind of innovation that makes the world go round, rather than the kind that turns it upside down, and a little can end up going a long way. But it is unglamorous compared with the dizzying ascent and overnight fortunes won by a select few under the Valley Way, and neglected by comparison. Let's call these the marathon runners.

The paths that marathon runners and sprinters follow are likely to be strikingly different, too. A sprinter may set out to build a billion-dollar company, but is more likely to build a piece of neat technology which they sell to one of the tech giants – assuming they don't simply flame out. Even the tech is not really necessary: in line with the dictum that investors back founders and teams, many sales are actually 'acqui-hires' where it is talent that is purchased, not a product or service.

For example, in 2015, a talented group of machine learning experts, recent graduates from University College London, decided to form a start-up under the name Bloomsbury.ai. They had no investment, no real product and no revenues, but they had developed a system for reading documents and answering questions about the contents. But testing that system's effectiveness required serious computational power – the kind normally the preserve of the likes of Google and Facebook.

As it happens, that was precisely what a Digital Catapult programme called the Machine Intelligence Garage could offer. The Garage is funded by a grant from the European Regional Development Fund, as well as Digital Catapult's own funds, and is intended to bring deep tech companies with well-defined business ideas and technical capabilities together in a neutral, technology-agnostic environment. Bloomsbury.ai duly joined the Garage and quickly demonstrated the value of its system, but had barely started to turn it into a product when the company was snapped up by Facebook. The company was dissolved and its fledgling product open-sourced, but Facebook had got what it wanted: engineering talent. It might seem a complicated way to go about hiring, but consider: at the time of writing, the average valuation of a skilled developer of machine learning software is around $1m, and assembling a productive team is a headache. If you are flush with cash, snapping up a company that has already done the hard work might look expedient by comparison.

The Bloomsbury.ai story ended in triumph for the engineers as individuals, and as a successful outcome for the Digital Catapult's Machine Intelligence Garage; but perhaps not the best outcome from the perspective of economic development: investment in UK academic research ended up boosting a top Californian company's fortunes. The Garage had served its purpose in a way, but how much better might things have turned out had a UK company partnered with Bloomsbury.ai, or if it had been able to scale up further before selling out? For all our efforts in this area, the drive to help companies to achieve scale is only getting started.

So much for the sprinters. What about the marathon runners? They may not be looking to sell out quickly – or indeed at all. People who want to do things a *little* better may be industry specialists – it's often hard to spot these kinds of modest but important improvements without deep domain knowledge – and content to make a comfortable living (and lifestyle) for themselves rather than making anyone filthy rich. They may also be motivated by passion for their field or a desire to tinker with interesting but ineffectual challenges. This is a common scenario at university spinouts.

Marathon runners may not welcome external investment, at least beyond the minimum needed to get off the ground. Instead they opt for the heroic simplicity of bootstrapping their business and building revenues slowly but (hopefully) surely. Refusing external investment means retaining control – over equity, the pace of growth and, most emotively, their destiny and that of their venture. It also means being able to ignore what might be an unwelcome reality check, and never having to take too big a risk, which is potentially appealing to those who might lack confidence in what they're doing.

The continued existence of marathon runners testifies to enduring (and growing) suspicion of the Valley Way: but slow and steady does not always win the race. Today, competition is almost inevitable, with market share and rapid growth critical to success in many sectors, particularly those that involve digital technologies. Investment allows operations to ramp up, headcount to grow and sales and marketing to aim high; forgoing it means giving up on the ability to compete effectively. Today, that often means not just being relegated to second (or third, or fourth) place, but facing extinction.

So which is better, sprinter or marathon runner? There's no straightforward answer: it depends on the founder's personality and the business opportunity. It is exhausting being a sprinter: you have to keep running just to stand still, as Uplister found out. Meanwhile, marathon runners can tire of the slow and steady course, with the finish line seeming to remain forever out of reach: the Finn brothers had spent their entire adult lives building up Sibelius before they brought in an outsider to speed their way to an exit.

And if there is a genuine opportunity, others will spot it. Sprinters are quick off the blocks, but will find it difficult to avoid being gobbled up by a GAFA wolf before they reach the finish line, as happened with Semetric. Marathon runners plod along, enjoying the experience at their own pace, but have to be careful not to be overtaken by swifter rivals. New technology or trends can also put them out of business: all the decades of investment the music labels had made in packaging and promoting discs were suddenly for naught when the kids decided, more or less overnight, that they were fine with downloaded mp3s instead.

In reality, of course, this division into marathon runners and sprinters is a caricature. A typical start-up is likely to switch from one model to the other, particularly as it picks up momentum and a logic of its own. Once a team is in place and people's jobs are on the line, a responsible CEO has to keep thinking about how to extend the runway, regardless of profitability. Ultimately, whether sprinter or marathon runner by inclination, the founder has to keep the machine running. That can be unsatisfactory for both: sprinters begin to feel they have less time to work on their world domination plans because they have to keep the sales flowing, or spend their time dealing with shareholders. Marathon runners feel they're losing touch with their passions, with the product and relationship development that they enjoy becoming a sideline to growing amounts of grunt-work.

Unless the business is to remain small, or occupies one of the increasingly rare niches where competition is limited and organic growth suffices, its initial funding will run down, and it will have to conserve cash. Then it's a hard uphill grind to get the next round in, generally meaning at least six months of distraction. Many start-ups will fail at this point. But even if they succeed, the new money doesn't make things any simpler: if anything, it makes them far more complicated.

Growing pains

{'Adhara', Mop Mop, *Lunar Love*, 2016}

Many start-ups get going with funding from the famous combination of fools, family and friends, who tend to invest out of trust when there is very little to go on. Later, they may turn to angels, who invest on the basis of intuition and whatever level of due diligence they find satisfactory when there is still not much hard evidence to go on. While the stakes may be personally significant, they are not so large as to attract intense scrutiny. But as the business gets bigger, it attracts 'serious' investors who are likely to make harder-headed appraisals of the management and the business, based on a proliferating set of metrics. Different kinds of investors – institutions, grant-givers and high-net-worth individuals, say – will have different requirements. But they will all push for change if they think it is needed.

I've met many inexperienced founders for whom that level of complexity is scary and who consequently seek to avoid investment of any kind. They are afraid that their own inadequacies as executives might be discovered and that they will be ousted from their roles, or at the very least that they will lose control over their businesses, particularly as heavyweight investors start to take up seats and voting rights on the board – like the tussle that took place when Paul Marshall wanted to take more of a hand in running Music Glue (Chapter 5).

This is not a groundless concern. The expertise and resources needed to get the business off the ground are not the same as those needed to run it as a going concern. As employee numbers grow and the number of products increases, the company will require a more process-driven approach – and that typically requires different skills, mindsets and experience. The CEO of a £100m business has a very different job to the CEO of a £20m start-up. The founding CEO may not enjoy this transition, or be capable of making it. So there is much to be said for bootstrapping a business up to a certain point. The longer you can go without taking investment, the stronger a position you will be in – up to a point.

But the fear of replacement or losing control should not be a deterrent to taking investment. In some cases, the founders will be well served by bringing in someone who has the experience they don't, as the Finn brothers did when they looked for a more experienced executive to run Sibelius. There will be others where things really do go wrong and a new CEO has to be parachuted in to save the day – but that is preferable to losing everything if the business goes to the wall. But most of the time, the investors appraise the incumbent team and back them if they like what they see. That hardly speaks to drop-kicking them out of the organisation at the first opportunity.

On the flipside, forgoing investment is often not a good idea. Even if a company has got some way along in its product development and perhaps secured its first customers, it will still need to firm up its position and scale up its operations. The fact is that if there is a market for your product or service, there will also be competition for it. The competition might not be as smart as you, and might not do things as well as you. But while you might be convinced that your way is a gazillion times better, the chances are that only some of your potential customers will agree.

Investors often approach high-tech businesses with a key question: what category are you in? This question is revealing in two ways. Firstly, because new and improved solutions to well understood problems are much easier to sell than solutions that anticipate problems that no one yet realises they have. Secondly, it is an inescapable truth about investors that they like to invest where others have invested before them. Investors want their portfolio companies to be radically innovative, but very few of them are anything like as innovative themselves. And history is full of examples of technically superior products that nonetheless lost out in the marketplace.

Any ambitious business will almost inevitably have to accept at some point that someone else is effectively calling the shots, to a greater or lesser extent. That might be an investor, but there needs to be a good fit: as we saw with Music Glue, the outcome when a marathon runner teams up with a sprinter (or vice versa) is not always elegant. If the parties are not in agreement on what constitutes 'good business', a sort of ungainly three-legged race results – at least until someone gets cut loose. Or it might be a big customer who wields the clout: as we found out at Semetric, the need to keep our anchor clients happy almost dictated the course of product development.

Figuring out when to make a transition, or take on investment, is more of an art than a science, and one which is heavily informed by experience. How fast to scale, and when, can literally be the billion-dollar question.

For two decades, the model has been the hockey-stick growth and stratospheric valuations of Silicon Valley success stories. While this was originally a somewhat startling development, it is now the default expectation for some investors, for whom the *only* way to think of the world is in terms of 'blitz-scaling'. These investors are on the lookout for companies who need to scale super-fast, usually to attack a global market where first-mover status is a clear advantage. Uber and Airbnb are two obvious examples of companies for whom the urgency of acquiring dominant share in as many territories as possible dominated their strategy from day one. However, this approach requires confident and aggressive investors as well as confident and ambitious founders. The UK has attracted the same level of venture capital investment over the last decade as the rest of Europe put together. But we still fail to produce major new players who grow into robust businesses at the centre of their markets.

This is at least in part due to the risk-averse attitude of the investment community. There are still relatively few UK investors compared with US investors, and they tend to be more conservative by nature. The level of investment is lower, and the investor confidence to follow on is much less common than in the United States. One of Silicon Valley's less noted but more salient features is its vibrant and successful ecosystem of reinvestment by serial entrepreneurs, and by the companies they founded. The West Coast has now seen two or perhaps three generations of digital business: there is simply more expertise there than in Europe or elsewhere. That lead is not unassailable, but it will take slow and steady progress for Europe to catch up. Overall, the depth and size of the funding community in the United States makes it an easier place to raise investment and to find ambitious, insightful experienced investors who will understand what you are trying to do.

Ironically, in my experience, angel investors are willing to come back with follow-on investment more frequently and consistently than their institutional counterparts, albeit typically for comparatively modest amounts. The latter are often deterred by their fiduciary responsibilities to their end investors, particularly if those ultimate investors are using public money: they are obliged to seek a return rapidly, rather than take the risk of staying in the business for longer and helping it scale.

So the single biggest problem for UK start-ups is that they are under-capitalised. This is the vicious circle in which European founders, CEOs, non-execs and investors all find themselves. It is a conundrum that some might argue could begin to be resolved by making public funding more readily available to build that investor confidence. That is certainly one of the goals of Digital Catapult.

Mousetraps and models

{'Mambo Sinuendo', Ry Cooder, Manuel
Galban, *Mambo Sinuendo*, 2003}

Whether a sprinter or a marathon runner, there is one question
that any aspiring entrepreneur must be able to answer if they
are to succeed, or just plain survive: how are you going to make
money? It's an obvious question, but it's remarkable how often
there's no obvious answer.

One answer is given by the old saying: if you build a better
mousetrap, the world will beat a path to your door. This is the
product design answer. It's not easy to build a better mousetrap these days, but digital technologies mean that there's room
to build improved versions of a host of other products. The
telephone, to pick an obvious example, has been transformed
from a single-purpose electromechanical device for talking to
people into a miniature, multifunctional digital computer used
for doing almost anything *but* talk to people.

The old saying is not wrong. Build a significantly better
product, and the world really will beat a path to your door. The
fact is that no one needed to have an app on their mobile phone
in order to order a taxi. Nobody needed to see how far away the
taxi was that was coming to collect them. But when Uber introduced those things and removed the need to hand over cash on
arrival at your destination too, it had a killer app. But there is
an infinity of creative possibilities to explore, and it is far from
obvious which ones will find market acceptance at any particular time. Some ideas are possible, at least in principle, decades
before consumers are ready to accept them: video conferencing,
for example, has been around for decades, but it took a global
pandemic to make it a commonplace. The circumstances under
which acceptance arrives are murky at best.

What often happens in practice is the logic of 'build it and they will come': make something sufficiently novel, and it will create its own market, as the iPod is said to have done. The problem is that all too often, what is built is functionality that nobody really wants or needs, and 'they' don't in fact come. This has happened repeatedly as digital technologies have emerged.

In the first wave, dotcom entrepreneurs spent fortunes on dedicated websites for every imaginable subject and commodity, only to see them fold in the face of all-purpose search engines like Google, compendiums of knowledge like Wikipedia and comprehensive marketplaces like eBay and Amazon. In the second wave, every imaginable object was connected to the internet, from speakers to doorbells. One of my favourite devices, which is always popular when explaining the internet of things, is the connected mousetrap. Once a prototype, there is now a £1,300 model brought to market by the pest-control company Rentokil which you can check out in Digital Catapult's Future Networks Lab. It saves companies like Rentokil a lot of money because a large element of the company's costs is in touring round umpteen traps to see which ones have been triggered and have an occupant, as it were. Being able to check on your app and visit only the triggered traps saves a huge number of wasted journeys. The company really did need a better mousetrap.

Now we are seeing 'smart' features that use artificial intelligence to do everything from drive your car to brushing your teeth. A few of these will indeed break through, mostly ones with corporate muscle behind them, although even then they can struggle. Amazon has succeeded in getting an Alexa into many homes, but its attempts to launch a phone flopped dismally, even though both served the same ultimate purpose:

removing friction from shopping. For whatever reasons – strength of competition being an obvious candidate – people were receptive to the speaker but hostile to the phone.

Perhaps it is because products are tricky that so much attention has been given to business models in recent years. Rather than *building* a better mousetrap, why not focus on finding a better way of *selling* mousetraps? Certainly, in the early days of the internet, this seemed a reasonable idea: e-commerce was a whole new sales channel, after all, and one whose rules were far from clear. For a while, it seemed more important to have a new, bold business model than a valuable product: you could even get a 'business process' patent for something sufficiently audacious.

The problem is that there really aren't that many ways to sell something even in principle, and fewer still in practice. You sell, you lease, you barter, you turn a service into a product or vice versa. That truth got rather obscured in the early days of the web, when 'information wants to be free' became a clarion call and the assumption that followed was that everything else online should be free too. As we've seen, music was the first to succumb to this, with MP3.com, Napster and BitTorrent demonstrating how music could be distributed for 'free'. And it wasn't just about music, almost every form of content – books, news, artwork, photography, films – all apparently 'wanted to be free'. It was a crude acknowledgement of a fact of physics which is that if you can consume a digital version of a piece of content, then you can also share it. Although digital rights management became an enormous industry trying to hold the finger in the dyke as it were, the reality of where we are today is that convenience and a great user experience are the best form of digital asset management (except when it comes to the blockchain, but we'll come to that later). During the first dotcom

boom, advertising funded all sorts of goods and services to consumers for free, including internet access itself. Most of those
services sank without trace, leaving the few victors Google and
Facebook to achieve their vast scale. Both had what appeared
to be free offerings but as it was famously put, if you're not
at the table then you're probably on the menu. The Facebook
and Google asymmetric business model where you give away
a service for free in order to charge others for the data arising
out of the consumer behaviour was for many years simply not
understood by most of the users of these services – which eventually was nearly all of us. It has a sleight of hand to it, which
eludes many. Even today, this kind of asymmetric transaction
does not appear in any GDP calculations of national economic
activity because the model doesn't fit traditional retail.

The genius of this approach was making the transaction
into a kind of unconscious barter. We give up the value of our
personal individual data without feeling any pain at its sur-
render. That lack of pain is gradually changing among users as
the risks of compromising our privacy in this way have become
more apparent, at least to some. But even then, it might not
have succeeded had it not been for another innovation that
turned a head start into a permanent advantage: the introduction of **platforms.**

Platform power

{'Alegntaye', Akale Wube, *Sost*, 2014}

A platform has a fairly specific meaning in computing, but in
this context I'm using it more loosely to mean a strategy for
delivering goods or services at scale – at such a huge scale, in
fact, that there is room for only one or two such platforms in

the world in each particular business sector. Most platforms are two-sided markets, connecting a large group of sellers with a large group of buyers and benefiting from network effects that make them increasingly unassailable from competition.

Music was, as ever, the bellwether. Napster supplanted the entire music industry practically overnight by allowing peer-to-peer file-sharing; Apple's legalised version of that was built on the hardware–software combination of iPod and iTunes, together with an unbeatable library of legitimate music files. But the truly transformational player was Spotify. Streaming on demand has no equivalent in the world of physical music sales (unless you count jukeboxes). And subscription payment was also new – the iTunes store was very much a transactional marketplace.

So far, so good. Spotify has made a lot of money for its investors and founders, and also for the music labels, which it has helped to snatch victory from the jaws of defeat. It is, by Valley standards, a 'good' business (even if it is based in Stockholm and New York, not San Francisco): rapid growth, vast market share and seemingly unassailable dominance over both creators and listeners. But there are two other respects in which it falls short of being a good business.

The first is that being a platform is expensive. Supporting all those apps and devices and suppliers and customers, and doing so better than anyone else, on a larger scale than anyone else, is not easy. It takes serious engineering and marketing, and those don't come cheap. So whether it is sustainable over the long term remains to be seen. Spotify has boasted handsome economics so far, but there are signs of pressure emerging as labels have started to ramp up their demands, even as it becomes harder to find new subscribers.

Recent dramatic drops in the Netflix share price are an

immediate reaction to the news that its subscriber base, post-pandemic, is shrinking not growing. This is hardly a surprise given the increased competition among streaming video services and the limited number of potential subscribers globally. In the face of a recession and rapidly rising living costs, and as people emerge from the pandemic and want to spend less time cooped up at home, cancelling a Netflix subscription is a logical step.

The second drawback to the apparent gloss on Spotify's model is that it makes its money at the expense of the music creators, many of whom have been reduced to digital peasantry with the collapse of the live scene in the pandemic. Much has been written elsewhere about the absurdly low amounts most songwriters and performers earn from Spotify. This is largely due to the fact that legacy artists on major labels are paid by the labels in ways that are determined by analogue contracts signed decades before platform services like Spotify, YouTube or AppleMusic were imagined. But it is also to some extent an inevitable feature of the platform model. Spotify's objective is not really to let people support their favourite artists, whether financially or otherwise: it is to act as the trusted intermediary that determines what you listen to.

There are signs this is beginning to change. The public mood is shifting as fans become uneasy about the lack of support for their favourite artists and even politicians in the UK have started to ask questions. Better deals for digital distribution of music are becoming available and major labels are beginning to ease back on some of their more punitive behaviours. Many artists who never recouped the value of their advances to labels are being forgiven those debts in an attempt by the labels to salvage their reputations ahead of governmental investigations into their business practices.

Lurking inside the whole legacy system is the emerging prospect of a new middle class of creators (musicians, artists, writers, craftspeople) who are starting to get paid for their work, because of the rise of the creator economy, initially via YouTube and Instagram and increasingly on TikTok. A range of platforms integrate creation, funding and distribution, some of which have been around for some time – like Music Glue and Bandcamp for musicians, DeviantArt for visual artists, and more generalist services like Patreon and OnlyFans, and SupaPass, supporting everything from newsletters to adult entertainment.

In addition the recent massive growth of interest and investment in platforms based on cryptocurrency which allow creators to tokenise the value of their products and services is taking things forward at breakneck speed. (We will take a closer look at the impact of blockchain and cryptocurrency in Chapter 9.)

There is also another new breed of platform that is empowering creators and their fans: games worlds. In *Minecraft*, *Roblox* and *Fortnite*, the point is to play games and, for some, to be the creator of your own game or environment. Some of these become hugely popular with other users of the site – in effect, crowdsourcing not just the funds for a creation, but the creation itself. They are designed not as social media, streaming site or creator monetisation, although they dovetail neatly with all these things. So, for example, there is a huge audience for videos of people building elaborate *Minecraft* creations or streaming their activities over Twitch.

These sites account for a rapidly growing proportion of the time our children are spending online. Being commercial enterprises, they have started to leverage their huge audience numbers and broadening their demographics by hosting incredibly popular content and events, notably the musical spectaculars attended by millions of fans in *Fortnite* – for example, the Travis Scott concert which attracted 12 million participants. In many ways, they have moved beyond being platforms towards being entire worlds, or even universes. So great is their influence that they are shaping up to be the new imperial powers of the digital landscape – pioneers of the metaverse. More on that later.

Do the right thing

{'Ballad of a Thin Man', Bob Dylan, *Live at Budokan*, 1979}

We've discussed how a business can be good for founders, good for investors, good for customers and good for creators. But a good business is also good for people. It is possible for a business to deliver good results for some or even all these groups and yet be bad for society. That's something that some of the Valley's swiftest sprinters have disregarded on their way to the finish line, whether it be Facebook attempting to redefine the entire concept of privacy or Uber playing dirty with regulators. But there is dwindling patience with this disregard for social norms, and growing scepticism about the benefits of this kind of disruption.

All technologies raise ethical questions – or at least, they do if they are more meaningful than connected mousetraps. And of today's emerging technologies, none raises thornier questions than artificial intelligence (AI), which by its very nature takes humans out of the loop. Letting AI do its own thing, with little regard for the consequences, has arguably led to some of the most deleterious outcomes of the sprinter mentality. The algorithms and machine learning systems in widespread use in both Google's and Meta's analytics systems are veiled in corporate secrecy but it is beginning to become clear that they are more likely to exploit people than empower them, more likely to enforce existing social prejudices than dispel them, and more likely to extrapolate search questions to extremes rather than take people back to a political centre ground. And the systems are still largely being left to offer up results and make decisions that are primarily driven by income potential without any consideration for the wider context. So video-recommendation algorithms end up radicalising their viewers and self-driving car systems get into accidents any human would see coming. A colleague on Sand Hill Road, home of Silicon Valley's venture capital companies, told me of an incident in which a senior executive in Meta approached Zuckerberg with a solution to the problem of embodying prejudice and bias in search results and content recommendations, but when the CEO saw that this would have a negative effect on income generation he rejected the proposal. The executive subsequently left the business.

In many cases, you or I might only dimly be aware of the systems at work, mostly through targeted adverts and the irritation of being offered products you have already bought or holiday destinations you have already visited. The reason for this is because consumers are not the ones who pay for the service. So how could they know whether the recommendations are the ones they want or need? And this is why it requires government intervention to regulate these behaviours: as all the operators' business models are much the same, the consumer's only option is to withdraw from using them altogether – but the reality is that the platforms would barely notice individual defections, so huge are these global user bases.

There are also problems when we are the objects, rather than the supposed beneficiaries, of algorithmic decision-making.

Inevitably AI is used to create answers to complex questions and the means by which those answers are generated can be subject to the prejudices and biases embedded in their designs and training data, as has been extensively documented. This takes on particular urgency when the machines find answers to problems in ways their creators do not understand. There is an urgent need for transparency and explainability. Digital Catapult has published reports on the work of its ethics team in helping new companies avoid the trap of building unconscious bias into new business models at a very early stage, which, as Meta is demonstrating so publicly over time, becomes increasingly difficult to unravel, even if you want to – which is an entirely separate debate.

Although many organisations have tried to work out how to create an ethical framework inside which to develop AI – notably Google in the United States and the Ada Lovelace Institute in the UK – none of them had the ability or the inclination to test how these might work in practice with start-ups attempting to developing ethical business models.

Because of Digital Catapult's work as an accelerator and a convenor of expertise around key technology areas, we work with hundreds of early-stage or scale-up companies every year, including about seventy a year that are selected to enrol in the Machine Intelligence Garage. The Garage provides access to the technical resources that AI start-ups need to prove their worth – primarily data and computational power – and facilitates relationship-building with peers, investors and industry. We thought we should complement this with assistance in navigating the often-complex ethical context for their work, and duly convened an Ethics Steering Committee, chaired by Professor Luciano Floridi of the Oxford Internet Institute's Digital Ethics lab. The committee undertakes deep dives into individual companies to explore the challenges, issues and solutions they are finding.

One of the companies we worked with early on was Loomi, a London-based technology company creating human-focused artificial intelligence. Having previously built digital solutions for some of the world's biggest brands, the focus of the Loomi team was on building a secure, ethical, private space for users and organisations to interact with information through personal AI assistants. Most such tools are voice-operated search engines or chat bots, but Loomi wanted to automate the tasks that a human personal assistant might otherwise carry out.

That meant it would not only have to be extremely reliable – nobody wants their smart assistant messing up their diary – but also extremely trustworthy. Not only would it have to adhere to the highest standards of information security, but it would also have to handle user data with rigorous care, and do so transparently. That integrity was viewed as key to winning users' trust – particularly in organisational contexts where it might have access to data on hundreds or thousands of individuals.

The Loomi team joined an early cohort of the Machine Intelligence Garage. Their initial focus was on functionality and finding ways to reflect the company's core values within the products and the business as a whole. Exposing themselves to an Ethics Committee deep dive proved to be a significant benefit, enabling Loomi to go into unprecedented detail, and enabling the exploration of a wide range of relevant aspects of product development, including meeting the needs of different types of users, establishing relevant policies, training, communications and marketing strategies.

As well as learning from industry and academic research, the deep dive enabled Loomi to focus dedicated time and expertise on this important area of the business. This facilitated questioning, reflection and prioritisation, resulting in changes to the product roadmap, such as relabelling functionality to make it more intuitive to the user, and finding different ways to evaluate sources of news content. Ultimately the team thought the process important enough to push back the launch to accommodate it.

Now there was a structure for implementing and managing ethics, and this output would be used to influence and differentiate the way Loomi's service is marketed. The Loomi team have continued to interact and network with others on the Machine Intelligence Garage cohort, and recently came back to contribute a successful Digital Catapult workshop to share learnings on AI ethics and algorithm transparency.

We still have a long way to go to find transparency in algorithmic design, to create forms of automated explainability, to have the machine vet itself. We are still at an early stage of the development of this kind of business. The mistakes and the challenges represented by the current tech giants are the typical errors of first movers writ large. The degree to which those companies are far ahead of others in developing their AI capabilities is matched only by the degree to which these ethical challenges are so deeply embedded in their businesses that they may never be able to extricate them without the brute force of outside intervention. I feel optimistic that better approaches will develop and that, through the intervention of governments in the United States and Europe, the time of the current tech giants will elapse and new players will enter the market and compete. The depth of feeling in the current generation of start-ups who walk through the door at Digital Catapult and their shared conviction that they must take an ethical approach from day one is growing. In the end, it's probably that sentiment rather than the interventions of governments that gives me the confidence to remain optimistic. As one wise voice put it, a Loomi that misuses your personal data is ultimately as uncommercial as a bank that misuses your money.

As we have explored the digital landscape, matters of a profound ethical and philosophical nature seem to come quickly and frequently to the surface. As we will explore in the final chapter of this book, future technologies will raise more such questions, from the proprieties of advertising in augmented reality to the morality of the metaverse. In these new realms, businesses will have to be even more vigilant about the ethics of their models, but it is inevitably a mixed picture. There are also plenty of young companies driving hard with no visible ethical compass and no sense of the direction they will go in, other than towards the money.

9

CULTURE CLASH

{'Clint Eastwood', Ed Case/Sweetie Irie refix, *Gorillaz*, 2001}

Digital Catapult occupies stunning glass-walled offices on London's Euston Road, the main thoroughfare for London's Knowledge Quarter. Our neighbours include Google, the British Library, the Francis Crick Institute and Universal Music. If you scan the view from the windows, you can see the topography of London laid out, from the Houses of Parliament to St Paul's Cathedral, the shiny new towers of Silicon Roundabout and the bucolic green pastures of Hampstead Heath. It is a panorama that invites visitors to consider the relationships between the state, the law, finance, knowledge and innovation.

The vista invites us to open our minds to the possibility of doing things differently, and that is certainly what we celebrate at Digital Catapult. Because so much innovation in the digital space takes place in start-ups and scale-ups as well as in universities, its engagement is more complex than those of its siblings in the Catapult network. There is comparatively little straightforward translation of academic research, and a much more diverse set of stakeholders. We talk constantly to all kinds of start-ups and scale-up companies, to established multinational companies, to private investors, academics and the government.

We engage with these stakeholders to identify their business and innovation needs, as well as to understand how they may contribute to key trends in policy making, such as the push to 'level up' the UK or the drive to reduce carbon emissions. It is critical to our success that we do not advocate any particular commercial or technological solution: instead, we create facilities, programmes or capabilities that help companies bypass or overcome obstacles to innovation and deployment.

That might mean a 5G test bed (of which seven have been built at time of writing), a 'factory of the future' prototype (like the one we created with the Advanced Manufacturing Research Centre and BAE Systems), or an experimental studio to produce immersive experiences (such as the ones we have built with Dimension, Imaginarium and Target 3D). These are funded in a variety of ways: in addition to our core grant from Innovate UK, we assemble consortia to bid for other research and development funding, as well as working directly with commercial players such as Verizon, Seagate or Niantic.

Digital Catapult programmes come in all shapes and sizes, but they tend to have two things in common. The first is that they go where private investment is not yet ready to tread – we continue to shoot ahead of the duck. After all, there would be no reason for the public sector to get involved otherwise: as I learned at the Technology Strategy Board, economic development requires that public expenditure brings 'additionality'. The second is that these programmes bring together people who wouldn't normally collaborate, from individual academics to giant corporations. It is these combinations of skills and expertise that are likely to find fresh approaches to old challenges and new opportunities.

When a well-known industrial supplier of gas to hospitals and labs came to see us one day, we were told that the company often wasted precious hours trying to locate its canisters to see if they needed refilling or replacing, and sometimes lost track of the canisters completely. We had recently been working with the Royal Air Force and the Navy on a similar kind of problem in which they sometimes lost track of the location and condition of items in their facilities. Using similar solutions, we were able to help the gas supply company place self-powered sensors on the canisters which could beam out their location to a low-powered wide area network and be mapped by a data collation and visualisation system that we developed. The result was an annual saving for its distribution business in the UK in excess of £10m a year. The supplier then rolled out the system across its territories around the world. It would never have encountered a group of engineers in asset tracking and the internet of things, and certainly would not have been able to benefit so quickly and directly from earlier R&D with the defence sector, but in this project with us, that's exactly what it got.

Digital Catapult's ambition is also to help prime industry for a net- zero future. The Catapult helps companies design for a circular economy and develop new business model propositions to transform the ways in which industry operates and contributes to environmental goals. A good example has been the support we have given to AI tech start-up Greyparrot in creating a compelling investor proposition. The founders identified that only 30% of the rubbish that is sent by consumers for recycling is actually recycled – because it is too expensive to hire people to sift the rubbish into different materials groups for processing. Greyparrot uses computer vision and AI to sort recyclable rubbish into material groups accurately and efficiently. As a result, it has generated more than £30m in investment, and was listed in the World Economic Forum's 100 most promising global technology providers in 2021.

Sometimes our work at Digital Catapult can seem like

science fiction come to reality. Imagine the challenges of autonomous air travel and freight. A large, slow-moving autonomous air cargo drone has flown into Belfast from New York. It has followed trade winds, risen and fallen with the barometer to minimise its energy use and carbon footprint. As it comes close to the Belfast Harbour airspace it is captured by a swarm of autonomous drone pilots which navigate it to land in the correct berth for unloading in the fully automated container yard. The drone swarm has full sight of all other air traffic in the region and can pilot down through altitude levels, calculating the timing and duration required to cross safely through piloted passenger traffic lanes. The drone swarm also has complete awareness of shifts and changes in the meteorological conditions to ensure stability, and optimised energy use is maintained throughout. On landing, the pilot drone swarm immediately reconfigures to begin the unloading process, summonsing the equally autonomous ground transportation vehicles as needed.

Digital Catapult, working with some major industrial partners, is designing a facility in Belfast that will enable the design and visualisation of this kind of system using combinations of AI and visualisation tools. The facility will create computer models of the whole complex system, digital twins, which will allow rapid prototyping of different approaches to designing and building every aspect of the system. It sounds like science fiction, but we are helping figure out what it will take it to make this real.

Another smaller example of a futuristic business we have supported is Extend Robotics. In maintaining massively tall telecommunications masts, the largest element of cost is in getting a service engineer to the site, making it safe for the engineer to climb to the top of a mast, and monitoring them on the way up and then down again. The shortest amount of time is spent switching a component in a control panel when the engineer is actually up there.

Wouldn't it be great if a robot could do the work at the top of the mast? That is the goal of Extend Robotics, led by Dr Chang Liu, of Imperial College London, who joined two Digital Catapult accelerator programmes to help develop his products. With careful engineering, it is possible to create a flying robot that can ascend a tower and clamp on to a surface with sufficient stability to carry out a repair. However, a high level of dexterity and control is required to manipulate a robot arm, equipped with a Philips head screwdriver, to remove a panel and switch out a circuit board, for example. The joystick controls on your average drone remote control are simply not sensitive enough to do the job, but if the controls of the arm are virtualised and mapped in virtual reality, you obviate the need for sensitive control, because you literally use a human hand to turn the head of the screwdriver. That's what Extend Robotics developed in Digital Catapult's immersive lab with help from our technicians. Extend Robotics has identified many practical uses of the technology in addition to this specific case, but telecoms mast maintenance alone is a £2bn market.

The kind of projects Digital Catapult excels at pull together amazing groups of people to face difficult challenges. Another such example is the 5G Festival project. The project aimed to crack a long-standing problem, which is the desire of musicians to collaborate with one another in real time over the internet. Lots of people have tried to do this, but the basic approach to packet switching and caching which lies at the heart of the internet's resilience is also the source of endless time lags of different lengths and unpredictable intervals. 5G Festival demonstrated very simply the way that super-low latency and ultra-high bandwidth can combine with 5G to overcome the challenges of geography and collaboration over the internet. Three groups of musicians were located in three different places: Brighton Dome on England's south coast, the 02 arena in southeast London, and Metropolis Studios in west London. More than 70 miles separated the musicians, but by creating a bespoke 5G environment, they were able to play together as if they were in the same room. Over two years they collaborated to pull off the feat that was enjoyed at the end of the project by a small pilot audience of 300 or so spectators in the three different locations. Some of the musicians received video feeds of each other playing fed into augmented reality glasses to enhance the remote collaboration experience. The musicians told us that so intimate was the sense of connection that when they came out for a break in rehearsals, they were looking around in bewilderment for where their fellow players were, before they remembered they were actually miles away in different cities. The programme brought together a major record label, Warner Music, several deep-tech start-ups with 5G network experience, specialist audio companies, venue owners, studio operators and the musicians themselves. The commercial opportunities awaiting the potential created here are for the companies to work through, but a few million of public investment has enabled that potential to be released and proven in the field.

Designing and developing digital solutions and facilities, creating and running programmes that bring diverse people together and allow them to get their hands dirty with the technology – these are some of the most beneficial aspects of what Digital Catapult does. The kinds of people with individual expertise who needed to come together in 5G Festival was as much of a challenge as solving the technical complexities. In some respects that kind of cross-sector collaboration is one of the most difficult challenges, because of a single factor: culture.

Squeezed out

{'Cler Achel', Tinariwen, *Aman Iman*, 2006}

The clash of cultures has been one of the defining themes of the digital revolution. Creators don't want to use their brains like businesspeople, and technologists are not usually motivated by the business models – at least not when they're creating. Ed O'Brien from Radiohead told me that when his band released *In Rainbows* on a pay-as-you-go basis, they found working out the economic arguments for doing it to be hugely interesting but a massive distraction. It wasn't that they couldn't do it, but it required them to be in a completely different headspace from making music. Similarly, the techies have been so preoccupied with, say, the challenges of streaming vast quantities of highly personalised data that they didn't think how those who made that data or content in the first place would ever get paid.

So the motives and incentives for the creatives, the suits and the techies are markedly different, and this gives rise to distinctly different cultures. This can go as far as physical separation: at the old Virgin Records Kensal Rise campus, the A&R team inhabited a separate building to sales and marketing – a creative tension that deepened when the maverick Virgin was bought up by the comparatively staid EMI. When digital entered the picture, there was literally nowhere for it to go: that's why, as EMI's new media guy, I ended up in the former financial controller's office at Capitol Records in LA: no one knew where to put me.

An accommodation was eventually reached, and both the

suits of the music industry and the smart casuals of the tech set prospered. But the new trilateral arrangement – business, technology and creativity – did not quite reach an equilibrium. Digital technology has enabled musicians' creativity to bloom in innumerable new ways but has also decimated the ability of most creators to profit from their works. Engineers, many of whom had a genuine love of music, had simply not developed the sophisticated notions of intellectual property and rights slicing that drives the music industry and ensured that musicians could make a living, even if they were ripped off along the way. There were, and are, glaring gaps and failures of communication between 'the people, the poetry and the pipes'.

This is not unique to the music industry. Digital books – ebooks – have not supplanted print to the same extent that digital music supplanted discs, but publishers and booksellers have largely ceded the online ground to Amazon and Kindle; having used books as a beachhead into retail, Amazon no longer seems particularly interested in exploring the potential of digital text. The large file sizes associated with video meant it took longer for film and TV to succumb, but broadband access was well on the way to making cinematic releases and scheduled broadcasts obsolete even before Covid-19 lockdowns left everyone with nothing better to do than binge on what are still anachronistically called box sets.

The clash of cultures started in the creative industries, and is most apparent there, but it is spreading. As more industries have been digitised – transport, office space, food delivery – their economics have been reshaped by the tsunami of money provided by venture capitalists and the like. We looked in the previous chapter at how this arises from a particular way of thinking about business – one that shows signs of becoming a monoculture despite its indifference to social norms. In this kind of environment, the interests of technology and of business become partnered closely and increasingly easily, and with little regard for anything but the quarterly results and the company's valuation.

There are signs that the tide is now turning against such single-minded businesses. But there is a degree to which most rank-and-file employees remain fated to be human cogs in algorithmically driven machines. They mostly have to make do as mostly powerless digital peasantry – from Amazon's delivery workers, unable to stop for toilet breaks, to Google's AI ethicists, apparently ousted for speaking truth to power. Occasionally, they muster enough collective strength to question working practices, but with job insecurity running rampant, most of these workers are simply glad of the pay cheque, regardless of the exacting terms under which it is earned. We have to ask what kind of culture is really at work in these businesses, despite their benevolent talk of changing the world. It increasingly seems as though the ends may have obscured the importance of the means.

There has been an insistence in some quarters that this represents the inevitable and necessary disruption of industries that had grown stagnant, failing to capitalise on the potential of technology to offer products and services that are cheaper and more convenient for customers and more efficient yet more profitable for the winning platforms. Indeed, one reason the GAFA titans have proved impregnable is because they can always point to the benefits they offer their customers: free-to-use online services, cheaper and faster shopping through greater choice, increased convenience in managing their work and domestic lives, and so on. Who could argue with that?

One answer is perhaps those who think there is more at stake than price and convenience. To go back to music, if you buy a track on Apple Music or stream it on Spotify, it is almost impossible to find out the names of the musicians performing, let alone what instruments they're playing, who produced the album or where it had been recorded. There are hardly any liner notes and the bare minimum of imagery, and the influences or inspirations for the work are left unspoken. In short, the geeky details beloved of generations of hardcore fans – which was transmuted into enthusiasm and transmitted to more casual listeners – have disappeared. The bulk uploading, distribution and consumption of music has been accompanied by a lack of respect for the musicianship and the craft of music-making.

Again, it's not hard to extrapolate to other industries. London's black cabs are worldwide icons: they offer safe, comfortable and reliable journeys – for a price. Uber, by contrast, is cheap and convenient, but nobody puts the average Uber Prius on a postcard (other types of car are occasionally available on Uber – especially if you pay extra). Similarly, staying in an Airbnb may have its advantages over a hotel room in terms of cost and convenience, but the premises rarely come equipped with a concierge, spa or room service. And Facebook's disregard for the tenets of journalism has allowed disinformation to run wild, with enormous consequences for debate and democracy.

Is there a better balance to be struck? One that balances the needs of creators and workers to make a decent living with the economies of scale and speed that digital offers? Or that recognises that some of what some tech giants appear to regard as inefficiency – editorial standards for disseminating news, for example – are in fact the checks and balances necessary to secure a greater good. Organisational culture is the way we assert and communicate what's important to us, so that when we encounter new situations or challenges we respond in a way that preserves our values and integrity.

The overweening influence of the Valley Way has eroded not just corporate cultures but social cultures too. Facebook was started by an engineer who wanted to remove all barriers to communication – any type of communication, at any cost. The obvious way to monetise this was to sell the data gathered to advertisers and marketers – any type of advertiser, any type of marketer. The results have included the persecution by WhatsApp of the Rohingyas in Myanmar, the Facebook-based Cambridge Analytica scandal in the UK and the deterioration of (particularly) young female Instagram users' self-image.

Facebook is perhaps the worst offender in this regard, but it is not alone. Google's corporate mantra of 'Don't be evil' long since became risible, while Twitter's own users refer to it as 'the hellsite'. Apple has recently positioned itself as a defender of privacy, but one suspects that is mostly to protect its own walled garden, which arguably has higher walls than any other. Now these titans are vying to maintain their supremacy as the new technologies that make up Web 3.0 are emerging, from artificial intelligence to virtual reality and all points between. Will they succeed? And if they do not, will their successors have learnt from their excesses?

Creative block

{'Angelo', Shai Maestro, *Shai Maestro Trio*, 2013}

In my thirty-odd years working at the forefront of digital technology, I have often found myself inhabiting a space that is simultaneously supremely optimistic and deeply cynical. A new technology is almost by definition flush with possibilities, and only time will tell which of those possibilities will turn into the next big thing. But through multiple cycles we have learned that the promise will either fizzle out or become all-consuming – and that either outcome can be problematic.

We are going through this phase now with many of our new technologies. Artificial intelligence is put forward as the solution for everything from drug discovery to global warming, but there is deep suspicion that its powers will mostly be put to work in order to further enrich billionaires and enslave workers. But perhaps the most contradictory field is cryptocurrency and distributed ledger technology – aka Bitcoin and blockchains.

Early discussion of Bitcoin promised a revolutionary alternative to conventional money. Because it existed only as digital tokens, 'mined' on a decentralised network of computers, it could be used anywhere by anyone in total anonymity. But because transactions were recorded perfectly and perpetually on the blockchain, this could be done with perfect assurance. No trust was required in anyone. A utopian world of perfect money and finance awaited.

People proclaimed that the blockchain would have the same kind of impact as the internet. In the early days of blockchain enthusiasm, people talked enthusiastically about the blockchain being like another layer over the internet but one that would be secure and transactional. Still more speculative was the linked concept of a smart contract, a piece of code that runs and executes actions based on a set of pre-agreed rules – completely binding but requiring no knowledge of the counterparties and no intermediaries. Two people or organisations could agree a deal and the smart contract would see to it that payment happened automatically as soon as its conditions were fulfilled.

Things turned out rather differently. The first that the

general public heard about Bitcoin and the blockchain was through the infamous Silk Road, a site on the 'dark web' that sold drugs and weapons, with no questions asked. Cryptocurrency quickly became associated with the dirtiest of dirty money, whether fairly or otherwise. Dirty in several senses: as well as its use by organised crime and other deeply unsavoury types, it quickly became obvious that mining the transactions to validate them on the blockchain creates an enormous and fast-growing carbon footprint.

Nonetheless, it was evident that the underlying technology was ingenious and potentially useful, but no one was entirely sure what for. I decided to tackle that question head-on when I was invited to spend a stint as an Industrial Fellow at the University of Glasgow's CREATe research centre. Given my background, the creative industries were the logical focus for my research.

It seemed that there were several potential applications in this area. The internet had it made it practically impossible to prevent copies of any kind of 'content' being made in limitless quantity and distributed and modified freely all around the planet. Not only did this make a mockery of copyright enforcement, but it also introduced more philosophical doubts about the nature of 'ownership' and 'theft': can you steal something if the original owner still has full use of it? What constitutes 'fair use' of a work, and how should a creator be compensated for its reuse or remix?

The Bitcoin blockchain recorded cryptocurrency transactions, but a similar distributed ledger could be turned to creators' advantage – at least in theory. Such a ledger could be used to establish, validate and track identities, so that individuals could be uniquely identified (for example, as the performer on a recording). At the grandiose end of the spectrum, it could be used to record the ownership of all rights in all recorded media, thus cutting through the mess of idiosyncratic records and databases that keep collective licensing companies busy and employing hundreds to maintain and trying to clean dirty data being generated on a global scale.

Or it might be used to reduce the cost of unit transactions, thus making licensing for very small sums viable and allowing creators in the 'long tail' – the large number of artists selling small numbers of product – to earn directly from their labours. Or to go even further, creators could specify that their work could be licensed for use in an online advertisement for any product except alcohol, tobacco or gambling, at a specified price and for a determined period in specified territories. That could be codified in a smart contract to automatically fulfil any request that met those criteria. In some ways this was flipping the model on its head; rather than a platform monetising creators' work through advertising, the creators themselves could monetise it through micropayments.

My research consisted of interviewing a wide range of individuals, from technology visionaries to the heads of the collecting societies, recording artists, music managers and label chiefs. Their responses reflected the mix of optimism and cynicism. Friends like the pop technologist and Harry Potter score composer Imogen Heap were seized by the revolutionary potential of the idea: she came up with the idea of the Creative Passport, a scheme for musicians to record their identities and works on a blockchain-like system. But others were more cautious. At best, they thought it had a long way to go to prove itself. At worst, Mark Meharry of Music Glue described the blockchain as the 'worst case of smoke and mirrors' he had seen in an industry that 'specialises in self-deception'.

Rather to my regret at that time I found myself agreeing

with the cynics, at least in the short term. In my evaluation, none of the start-ups then operating in the space was likely to gain critical mass, and I couldn't see the likes of Spotify or Apple replacing their technology with blockchain-based alternatives. And even if blockchain did reduce transaction costs enough to make it possible for creators in the long tail to start earning money from their work, I feared that would have the same effect as the earlier boom in exposure from the web and social media: far more creators competing for the same pool of attention. The expenses of marketing and promotion to rise above the noise would outweigh any cost efficiencies on the transactional side. Despite all the excitement around non-fungible tokens (which we'll discuss shortly), I suspect that this challenge is becoming even greater as more platforms enable more content creators to do their thing.

But beyond the short-term hype, blockchain clearly had the potential to meet a need that wasn't going away. I could imagine a coalition incorporating creative, technology and licensing organisations using decentralised ledger systems and other technologies to renew the basic architecture of the music industry for the 21st century. (Or, in a less utopian vision, multiple industry coalitions creating competing, non-interoperable architectures.) In fact, pieces of such an architecture were appearing even as I wrote my report: for example, 2016 saw the foundation of the Open Music Initiative (OMI), led by the Berklee College of Music and MIT Media Lab, with an impressive list of members.

The OMI is still working on an open-source protocol to allow rights-holders to be identified consistently across different platforms. That might seem an underwhelming rate of progress, but in fact it speaks to the often-overlooked truth that whereas blitz-scaling might work for businesses, infrastructure takes time to build. After all, it has taken more than twenty years for the world wide web and the mobile web to form themselves into a seamless and essential infrastructure for global economies. In fact, slow, step-by-step progress could also help to avoid the repeated failures that have marked previous attempts to create a digital infrastructure, when short-term business goals always got in the way of longer-term attempts to achieve more strategic benefits in a world weary of 'disruption'. It does not seem unreasonable to think that it could take ten to fifteen years to knit together this new layer out of new standards, protocols and systems.

As always, since music tends to be on the front lines of the digital revolution, we might expect other creative industries to follow. Digital Catapult worked closely with the Games Fund on a project to use blockchain to capture the creative contribution of games designers at the early stages of a collaboration. The idea recognised that individual creators often start something quite casually and only later does that project turn into something of value. By the time that happens, contributors forget who did what work and may have drifted off into other projects. If, however, you could memorialise, permanently on the blockchain, the contribution of a designer or lighting engineer with an agreement as to what share of the equity each had contributed, then even if they all fall out and have 'creative differences', those apportionments could still stand. The project was a partial success although we had to wait until one of the participating companies had genuine creative differences before we could really test it.

Since then, numerous other trials have taken place via the team at Digital Catapult working in sectors including nuclear decommissioning and construction. These projects are progressively teasing out how to make this technology work for businesses, even if not in the way originally conceived.

In the early versions of blockchain discussions, it was the trust-less arrangements that had the most exciting and most disruptive potential. These proposed architectures incorporated mining by the network to ratify the validity of a transaction and thus secure it. Miners were independents who ratified transactions by solving complex mathematical problems thrown up by the blockchain as a result of a transaction; when a sufficient number of miners arrived at the same answer, the transaction was authorised and inscribed on the blockchain. As the number of transactions on the blockchain increased, the complexity of mathematical puzzles to solve increased. This is the reason for the massive and exponentially growing energy consumption required by the blockchain. Most of Digital Catapult's experiments have been in trusted environments where the energy-hungry mining process is not required because the parties already trust each other.

Now another infrastructure has sprung up, which rewards creators for their work in a more freewheeling and potentially revolutionary way. Non-fungible tokens (NFTs) record that someone has claimed or purchased something – an image, a popular tweet, a meme, on a blockchain, theoretically in perpetuity and for all the world to see.

Perhaps the global Covid-induced lockdown accelerated this. But the recent explosion of interest in NFTs is attracting so much investment that it will last longer than a bubble, even if much of it is speculative and possibly shady. The buyer of an NFT has generally bought a thinly defined right to a piece of purely digital intellectual property with that claim being recorded on a blockchain for all to see, theoretically in perpetuity. Suddenly tweets, video snippets and ancient memes are being associated with NFTs that are achieving spectacular prices, most notoriously the sale for nearly $70m of a collage made by the previously obscure digital artist Beeple.

Although we might applaud this increased appreciation and valuing of cultural capital, there remains a great deal about the trade in NFTs that provokes concern. An NFT does not intrinsically give its owner any control over the asset: it can still be duplicated, shared and even sold again without the owner's permission. The eye-watering prices are generally paid in crypto-currencies at eyebrow-raising exchange rates. Many participants have declared interests and some have undeclared interests in talking up their trades and the value of transactions in their currencies. And there are a good number of NFTs that seem to blink into existence just long enough for someone to collect their crypto-currency earnings before disappearing again. However, despite the dodgy offerings, wallet hacks and general shadiness, the growing numbers of portfolios of NFTs on display on portals like OpenSea seem to be pointing to the emergence of a new digital asset class whose value is increasing and which ultimately seems likely to stick around simply because of its scale.

It is small wonder that NFTs are seen by many as the ultimate bubble, not to say an outright scam. And yet this development does hold promise for creators. The tokenising of creator platforms is increasingly seen as a new kind of community play in which the federated nature of a distributed autonomous organisation (DAO) allows for the establishment of new markets for tokens that can be governed transparently and ethically. If options and equity drove Web 1.0, it will be tokens that incentivise and finance Web 3.0. The great value is that there is an immediate market for NFTs, unlike options on equity which in the disillusionment of the post-dotcom boom were often useless paper. With tokens, creators do not need to wait for some public market liquidity event that might never happen. Instead they have an asset which is immediately liquid and the only question is whether to hold or to sell.

So despite the shady origins of the blockchain and the bubble-like nature of current investment levels, NFTs are more than an amusement for people with more money than sense. They also reflect a general increase in social acceptance that artists need to be paid fairly, which this technology enables. They may point the way to a potentially robust way of tying digital creations to their originators and of a more distributed form of digital patronage. Whether that will benefit most creators, or continue to favour a chosen few, remains to be seen. But the sheer quantity of investment pouring into this space suggests that some permanent value is being created that will not evaporate when the bubble bursts.

Beyond reach

{'Cool Struttin'', Sonny Collins, *Cool Struttin'*, 1958}

The evolution of the blockchain space perhaps points to the way other future technologies will develop, with unequivocally legitimate, socially productive activities sitting alongside others whose morality and social value are debatable, often indefinitely so. Although the authorities have started to pay attention to the most flagrantly illegal uses of cryptocurrency – including money laundering, black market trading and tax evasion – there is still much activity that is not only ungoverned, but that no one knows how to govern.

The trade in NFTs, for example, is difficult to regulate. If people want to spend vast amounts of money on intrinsically worthless pictures of apes, should anyone stop them? Going a step further, does it matter if the values of NFTs are propped up by self-dealing and artificially high valuations? When Damien Hirst failed to sell his diamond-encrusted skull on the open market, he bought it himself, with a couple of partners, presumably to maintain his value as an artist. Why shouldn't NFT creators do the same?

There has been a series of 'hacks' in the fledgling world of smart contracts and the decentralised autonomous organisations set up on the back of them. These organisations are meant to do what their charter says automatically, without room for error. But in several instances, people have found loopholes that instruct the DAO to pay them large chunks of their money. The other members and owners have been predictably furious, but it is not clear that there has been any wrongdoing. After all, as the US technology lawyer Lawrence Lessig once put it, 'code is law'. If the smart contract allows it, it's fair play. But undoubtedly the pressure to fix these flaws will grow and a tokenised creator economy is rapidly emerging in a way that is starting to look exciting.

Recent history suggests that charting a path out of this situation will be a long and messy affair. A quarter century after the introduction of the world wide web, we have not found a magical technological fix or legal silver bullet for its ills. Instead, we have a piecemeal collection of new laws and codes of conduct, together with a gradual shift in social norms that is slowly turning into changes in policymakers' stances. But we have no real consensus on how to deal with everything from file-sharing to freedom of speech on the internet.

Meanwhile, companies have continued to act first and ask for permission later – Uber and Airbnb come to mind – although there are now signs of a pushback in both the United States and Europe. But it is rare for those debating and drafting new legislation to understand the detailed issues at stake, or to anticipate the potential effects of any changes they may be contemplating. When tech bosses speak to politicians, legislators and policymakers, they often face naïve, soft-ball questioning that's easily deflected – or just decline to turn up, as a reminder of where the real power lies.

In the UK, laws are written generically, and often rapidly, on the basis that the necessary detail and granularity will come out by being tested and precedents created in court. Unfortunately, in the vertiginous digital world, the rate of change is so rapid that precedent may become increasingly difficult to apply. On what cases do you found the law when the situation is unprecedented?

The result is laws that are bad, or that cannot be implemented. As we saw in Chapter 4, the UK's Digital Economy Act was a knee-jerk reaction to the challenges of file-sharing, formed largely by the complaints of large film studios and major record companies and forced through over the objections of those who would have to enforce it. As a result, most of its provisions were ultimately abandoned as either impractical or redundant. At time of writing, the UK government is pushing through a bill intended to ensure that companies act to remove 'legal but harmful' material from their services – even as ministers still use Twitter to make fake assertions about their political rivals. It seems unlikely that this woolly set of provisions will work out any better than the Digital Economy Act.

When it comes to policy, the GAFA companies wield formidable power through 'lobbynomics' and public relations, much as big business has done since time immemorial. More insidiously, though, they also have the ability to shape public discourse, knowingly or otherwise, through their own products and services. Politicians are torn between fearing the power of social media to mobilise the public against them (as has happened in repressive regimes around the world) and wanting to use that power for themselves (as Donald Trump did with Twitter, and the UK Vote Leave campaigners did with

Facebook). It is probably for this reason more than any that Elon Musk chose to acquire Twitter in the latest twist and turn to the febrile story of the tech world.

The investor-driven desire for growth at any cost, and access to effectively inexhaustible reservoirs of cash, mean that tax regimes and consumer protections exist largely to be avoided. A business dealing in intangible goods can be domiciled wherever is most convenient; in the gig economy, occupancy limits or driver licences can be ignored, safe in the knowledge that the rules are virtually unenforceable. Attempts to make tech giants pay their taxes or obey local regulations are hampered by geographical constraints that are often easily ignorable on the internet. If it comes to it, the platform can mobilise its customer base and technology against the enforcers: Uber notoriously deployed variant versions of its app to foil attempts at monitoring its behaviour.

The result is that the influence of the digital city-states now rivals that of nation states. Mark Zuckerberg has a hotline to the White House; Jeff Bezos is worth more than Qatar. But governments still have power, even if it did take the combined might of the European Union to change the way companies handle private data, with the General Data Protection Regulation. At time of writing, the US Department of Justice had announced an anti-trust lawsuit against Google, accusing it of operating an illegal monopoly in search and search advertising. The licences of Huawei and TikTok to operate have become levers in the struggle for global supremacy between China and the United States, while China's own ecosystem of websites and apps rival anything coming out of the Valley when it comes to user numbers. And much of the Chinese internet is explicitly designed to facilitate social control by the government.

All this reveals increased willingness on the part of

governments to enlist tech companies in their domestic and foreign affairs without regard for how it affects consumer experience or advancement. We can all debate whether teenagers' obsession with TikTok was such that we should be grateful to Donald Trump for his attempts to outlaw it, but his interference – and the promises of his political colleagues and rivals to rein in the GAFA companies, in different ways – raise profound questions about the kinds of controls that are becoming politically acceptable. Given how dominant the GAFA quartet is, the impact on individual giant companies may not be readily distinguishable from the impact on the entire internet.

Of course the analogy goes only so far: Google, Amazon, Facebook and Apple don't make laws (although they lobby hard for them), they don't fight wars (at least not yet) and they provide brilliantly useful products and services (although it is the supposed 'customers' who are sometimes the product). But nonetheless it is not an exaggeration to say that the digital revolution that transformed the world did so in ways that were medieval in character.

For the moment, those giant companies – not just the internet companies, though they are the most obvious targets – seem untouchable, as do the elites they support and create, while the lives of ordinary people seem more precarious and disempowered. This growing gap between the perceptions of people on the street and those who would seek to create meaningful governance is a recipe for social unrest – a gap being prised wider by malicious actors ranging from state-sponsored trolls and hackers to conspiracy theorists to Cambridge Analytica, with both inadvertent and deliberate misinformation and disinformation making it harder for people to agree on even basic premises about their societies.

This suggests an alarming picture of the inability of

existing systems of governance and political regimes to contain the growing turmoil provoked by rapid socioeconomic change, which is itself driven by new technological capabilities that seem increasingly at odds with what the law is able to contain. Social media platforms are not intrinsically subversive, but they enable public sentiment to be organised, disseminated and amplified at scale, responding dynamically in real time to changing circumstances. Isolated incidents can spawn entire movements seemingly overnight, as demonstrated by #MeToo and #BlackLivesMatter.

Whether one approves of the individual causes is somewhat beside the point: such rapid deployments and realignments of social pressure are inherently destabilising. Technology built to disrupt commerce has ended up being used to disrupt entire societies. It could be debated whether the UK public would ever have voted in a referendum for Brexit, if it had not been for the insidious influence of the main social media platforms Facebook and Twitter – and while we're dishing out blame, let's not leave Reddit and LinkedIn out of this. Whether the current anti-trust lawsuits against Google and Facebook will act as a corrective to these tendencies remains to be seen, but one thing that's certain is that legislative change will come slowly, whether in the EU or the United States. Meanwhile, technology, and the companies built on it, will continue to run ahead of politicians and policymakers.

Return to core values

{'Yillah', Hadouk Trio with Steve Shehan, *Air Hadouk*, 2010}

During the cyberpunk-steeped infancy of the world wide web, the culture was one of optimistic libertarianism: there were few rules about what you could and couldn't do, but the overarching sentiment was positive. We expected the world not only to be aided by digital technology but also to be transformed by it – and the assumption was that this transformation could only be for the better. All we needed to do was follow Google's mantra 'Do no evil'. After all, the new technology offered essentially free, boundless and instantaneous communication; then limitless access to the world's cultural riches; and then the ability to redirect and reshape business, politics and society itself. What could possibly go wrong?

Today, that unbounded optimism seems naïve. The belief that things would work out for the best – that it was fine to 'move fast and break things', in Mark Zuckerberg's phrase – encouraged disdain for the way things were and unwarranted confidence that the outcome would be a net positive. Far from feeling liberated, many of us now feel oppressed by digital communication, which seems to have widened rather than narrowed the divides in our societies. The fruits of digital technology came at a price – paid by creators and perhaps, in diluted form, by the rest of us too. And it turned out that malevolent autocrats could use the digital tools to reshape politics and society at least as easily as democratic movements, if not more so.

But as the sense of power being concentrated in a very few hands has grown, so too has the feeling that *nobody* is in control. Kevin Kelly, the founding executive editor of *WIRED* and trusted guide to the early web, has argued that technology effectively behaves like an organism, seeing it as manifesting a kind of collective unconscious that exists beyond the deliberate actions of individual companies and governments. He suggests that there are innate drives in particular technological directions – increased processing power, say, or sharing and collaboration – that are collectively induced, rather than objectively directed.

Kelly proposes that the same application of a technology might emerge and propagate in different parts of the world without any direct link between contributors. This is the antithesis of the story often told about technology, in which an individual genius – say an auteur like Steve Jobs – conceives and minutely controls every aspect of an innovation. This idea of technology as a self-directing force, or even a kind of life form, may seem faintly absurd but I have a slightly unnerving conviction that it has some substance.

Was there a concerted plan that accompanied each of those waves of change that swept over first music, then retail, then services and most recently manufacturing? If there was, it was well concealed. To me it looks more like a pure chaotic gold rush each time: freemium offerings, subscription services, apps and now smart assistants and augmented services. The twenty-five years since the world wide web first appeared have been marked by a recurring pattern, in which individuals and small groups gain the tools to become entrepreneurs, using the internet as a lab where new value chains can be constructed, new products developed and new business models devised. Most of the time, the disruption that followed – despite often being celebrated for its own sake – has had unforeseen consequences.

Now it feels as though that disruption has broken free of the internet to threaten the fundamental operating principles of our society. Can we fix this situation? Even as we feel the technology is running out of control, we also feel as though everything is becoming more locked down. A handful of giant companies control the tools and technologies that increasingly dominate our lives, but seem either powerless or indifferent when it comes to their effects.

In a cyberpunk novel, that's where the renegades would come in, hacking together ways to route around the corporations and forge a new, anything-goes future. In reality, by contrast, everything is monetised and organised, right down to the blocks of code that are assembled into today's software and every step of the long supply chains that bring us even the most mundane of products and services. What was once the source of revolutionary possibility is now the source of mainstream global monopolistic behaviour. The masters of the universe deploy technology to serve their own ends; once in the wild, their technology does what it wants with us and to us.

But this dystopian picture isn't the only way things can turn out. We have seen how the introduction of a values-based approach is becoming more prevalent. If we are capable of collectively inducing trends in technology, we can induce them to be different, and the emergence of every new wave of technology affords a new chance to do that – to examine how we are using the tools to forge our new world, and to change the way things work. In our final chapter, we'll see how we might do just that as the clean lines between digital and reality start to disappear in Web 3.0.

10

BACK TO REALITY

{'The Silent Flight of the Owl', Manu Delago, *Circadian*, 2019}

At the dawn of the web, almost everybody viewed the internet as a separate realm, somewhere quite distinct from the real world. Indeed, that was part of its cyberpunk appeal: there were no rules about what was possible or how you might conduct yourself. And that remained true until it turned out that this freedom could end up costing established industries an awful lot of money.

At that point, many of the rules governing the online realm were the same as those everywhere else: lawyers, corporations and plutocrats dictated what was acceptable, even if piratical fringes and murky underbellies persisted. But even so, the perception remained of the digital realm as 'somewhere else'. You might no longer have to wrestle with crackling modems or getting cables laid, as we did in the 1990s, but throughout the noughties it still required substantial effort to get online – and once there, your activities were constrained by bandwidth and processing power.

That sentiment still rang somewhat true when Digital Catapult began operations in 2013. But over the next few years, the gap between the physical and the digital grew narrower. Mobile broadband and increasingly ubiquitous Wi-Fi made it easier for people to log in wherever and whenever they wanted, while the web (and particularly social media) had become increasingly participatory – somewhere to post and interact, rather than search or surf. That trend continues and is likely to accelerate as future networks increase the availability and capabilities of internet access.

So the digital realm is no longer 'somewhere else'. Increasingly, it is right here, all around us, all the time. Nor is it a medium for passive consumption: yes, we can play music and watch videos, but we also chat with friends and argue with strangers, send pictures of lunches and sunsets, flirt with dates and vent our hates, order taxis, meals and shop for everything. Almost every facet of human life can now be conducted partially or entirely online, and most of us, most of the time, can be readily identified (and tracked) by our digital trails. In short, the digital realm is no longer somewhere we go to escape our real lives. Increasingly, it is where our real lives are spent.

The city centres of the United States that were hollowed out by waves of suburbanisation in the 1970s and 1980s had started quietly to restore themselves in the early 2000s with dreams of artisanal, hipster regeneration. But two years of a global pandemic followed by a worldwide recession with eerie echoes of the 1920s and 1930s, has wrecked high streets and shopping malls across the globe as the habit of online shopping even for clothes and shoes has taken its toll on retail everywhere.

One telling measure of how 'real' the digital realm has become is how willing people are to spend money not just on e-commerce for physical things but also on things that have no physical existence. Games players have been happy to spend real money on digital power-ups for at least two decades. Entire economies have sprung up, initially transacting by means of in-game currencies but later fungible (or at least purchasable) with real-world money. Linden Lab's *Second Life*, launched in 2003, pioneered an online world in which people could buy special items for their avatars, as much for reasons of aesthetics or collectability as anything else, since it was more of a place to hang out than a game. That trend has continued through *World of Warcraft* and *FarmVille* on Facebook, into modern shared worlds like *Minecraft* and *Fortnite*, with NFTs being its latest and perhaps purest incarnation. That people are willing to spend fortunes on pictures of bored apes indicates how narrow the gap has become between conceptions of real and virtual assets. Acquiring digital assets confers more than bragging rights on Twitter. As digitisation removed physical books and music from people's physical bookshelves at home and eroded their visible cultural identity, NFTs and other digital assets are becoming the next generation's digital cultural identity, browsable on OpenSea or similar portals.

The reification of the digital realm was already well underway when I joined Digital Catapult in 2016. As described in Chapter 7, we ran a rapid strategy review and eventually decided to concentrate on the creative and manufacturing industries and driving early adoption of selected digital technologies with high potential. One such technology became obvious because of the UK's existing strengths in film, TV, games development and special effects, music and theatre. These all combine in immersive technologies – virtual reality, augmented reality and all the other ways of placing people inside a partially or completely simulated environment.

The basic appeal is obvious: today for most people the digital world still lives within a fixed view screen, whether that screen sits on your desk on in the palm of your hand. And most of the time we interact with it using just the tip of one finger, or perhaps twiddling our thumbs if we're texting. But we have been trying to make our experience of media spatial and tactile almost since the dawn of media. Initial experiments in placing sounds within a stereo field were followed by 3D film, multi-channel surround sound, haptic feedback in games, and so on. There is serious research into digital smells and tastes and how olfactory molecules can be digitised and reproduced. Now, with huge investments leading to rapid improvements in display technology, audio-visual effects and processing power, we are in a position to start creating entire worlds that are indistinguishable from reality. And with that, we could return to the cyberpunk fantasy of virtual realms beyond our own, where everything is possible and anything goes.

Building worlds

{'Aisatsana', Aphex Twin, *Syro*, 2014}

Our whole life is a battle against gravity. We struggle against it to stand and walk, fight it to a standstill for the bulk of our lives, but always ultimately concede defeat sooner or later, and return to our permanent rest in the horizontal. No wonder that one of the most enduring and universal of human fantasies is to be able to fly. From Icarus to Leonardo, the Wright Brothers to SpaceX, we have expended enormous creativity to escape gravity – and our earthly concerns – first through storytelling, more recently through heavy engineering. But now there is a new way to take flight, and it doesn't so much as require you to leave your living room.

In 1982, Microsoft launched the first version of its *Flight Simulator* software – three years before it launched Windows – to soar-away success. A decade later, the latest version landed on my desk at Virgin Records, at about the same time that I was developing my addiction to the internet. The flight simulator came on a CD-Rom, the only format capable of supporting its rich content, and we were blown away by its attention to detail and the effort to recreate the experience as closely as possible.

Flight Simulator continued to be a big seller for decades, and was joined by other simulators, notably the family of sandbox games beginning with *SimCity* in 1989. Today, almost anything you can think of has a simulator. As well as relatively conventional fare of train driving, fast food preparation and dating, you can, if you wish, live the amusingly anarchic life of an omnivorous goat or, for some unfathomable reason, experience the mind-melting tedium of driving for hours on end across a featureless desert plain.

Simulations aimed to recreate the real world, more or less faithfully, through sophisticated engines for visualisation, physics, basic social interactions, and so on. But once those existed, they could equally well be applied to the creation of *imaginary* worlds, designed to be convincing, but not faithful to any real-life experience. Text-based adventure games, leaving the players' imagination to do the heavy lifting, gave way to two-dimensional labyrinths and then to point-and-click environments that offered the illusion of depth and were filled with inhabitants unlike any to be found on earth. Eventually they too became shared space in which multiple players interacted online, beginning with *Neverwinter Nights*, which launched on AOL in 1991. And as these digital worlds grew more sophisticated, the range of activities they supported grew larger, evolving from combat to trade to conversation and creation.

It was not surprising that this coincided with the ascendancy of cyberpunk, whose protagonists jacked into virtual realms as a matter of course – notably in Neal Stephenson's 1992 novel *Snow Crash*, in which he coined the term 'metaverse' for an immersive successor to the internet. Stephenson's book was a key text during my early exploration of the internet (see Chapter 1), and the metaverse has remained as an enduringly appealing idea. It was clear, given the direction of travel, that we would sooner or later be able to create completely immersive environments that you would not so much navigate as inhabit. Why limit yourself to creating a website, when you could create a whole virtual world and play God?

Well, one reason is that going beyond two-dimensional screens turned out to be a matter of 'later' rather than 'sooner'. While massively multiple online games became more graphically sophisticated, attempts to make them more immersive, engaging the senses more comprehensively, proved tricky. Our evolution-honed bodies and senses are immensely sophisticated, and getting them to accept digital simulacra as real is correspondingly difficult. So although there were numerous attempts to make virtual reality hardware in the 1990s, the experiences they offered were unconvincing and disorienting, or even nauseating.

Enthusiasm eventually burnt out, as did the technological possibilities, so for most of the noughties, virtual reality (VR) lay neglected, while the comparatively accessible world wide web became the omnipresent manifestation of the digital realm. But the sector reignited when Palmer Luckey, a teenage hardware enthusiast, started a Kickstarter campaign for a new VR device in 2012, backed by games industry luminaries. Luckey raised nearly ten times his target; within a couple of years, his start-up, Oculus, had been acquired for more than $2bn by Facebook, which saw immersive spaces as the successor to social media.

Luckey's brainchild, the VR head-mounted display Oculus Rift, finally saw the light of day in 2016, the first of a new wave of VR devices from numerous manufacturers. These included everything from Google's simple Cardboard adaptor for smart-phones to professional rigs costing thousands of dollars. The technology was dazzling, but consumers remained uncon-vinced. One key problem was the lack of a killer app, or even much compelling content. For all the wow factor of a first encounter with virtual reality, it lacked durability: no one was sure what to do with it that justified the faff and expense.

So the nascent immersive industry ended up in a vicious circle, despite its undoubted potential. Headset manufactur-ers like Facebook, Sony and HTC Vive could not sell enough VR headsets, because there was not enough interesting content to justify their high retail prices. And not many people were interested in making content because not enough headsets were being sold to make it worthwhile. As time went on, and dis-enchantment grew among potential consumers, creators and investors, the circle showed signs of turning into a death spiral.

That was something we thought the Catapult could help avert. The UK couldn't compete on the hardware front – it was no longer a significant player in consumer electronics – but it punched well above its weight in storytelling and content crea-tion through its historic cultural strengths in these areas. Most forms of media take a while to settle into popular formats: it took a couple of decades for TV shows to stop being filmed plays, for example. We thought VR content needed a bit of time and space to experiment – time and space that it was perhaps not getting in the pressure cooker of Valley investment and games development. There were already many little experi-ments in VR content development, but what was needed was someone to pull it together, provide seed funding for interesting projects and companies and help the burgeoning sector to gain critical mass. We thought we could do that.

So in September 2017, Digital Catapult teamed up with

Arts Council England to establish a 12-week accelerator programme called CreativeXR, which enabled twenty winning companies every year to prototype cultural experiences using different permutations of VR, augmented reality, mixed reality and extended reality. Three years later, it had financed and supported the development of sixty immersive prototypes by leading UK creators with £1.2m and awarded production funding worth £850,000 to 12 of those projects, allowing them to create fully fledged production versions, often with match funding from industry.

The programme yielded an exciting range of experiences, ranging from interactive detective stories to experimental theatre, and from an empathetic exploration of paranoid schizophrenia to dancing with a virtual partner of more than a century ago. And our graduates picked up plaudits at festivals like Tribeca, the Venice Biennale and SXSW, with several, such as Madrid Noir and Goliath, being production funded by HTC Vive or Oculus and making it all the way to publication and availability for purchase on the Oculus and Vive stores. We couldn't yet claim to have learnt how to fly, but we had at least started to spread our wings.

Virtually there

{'Virtual World', Verve, *A Storm in Heaven*, 1993}

A simulated world can be beautiful to look at, full of sights and sounds to delight eye and ear. But it will fail to satisfy our basic human need for interaction if it is empty of other people, or at least decent impersonations of them.

Initially, people exploring simulated worlds like those encountered digital characters built like any other graphics, usually equipped with a few scripted lines of dialogue and some basic behaviours. As graphics and AI improved, they became more convincing, sometimes drawing on the recorded movements of human performers and able to act autonomously, albeit in extremely limited domains. But they still fell all too often into the 'uncanny valley', with hair and skin that seemed to be made of plastic, an inability to make eye contact and a tendency to make ungainly movements and try to walk through furniture.

In addition to wanting to fund content, we wanted to support companies in the immersive space. So we set up Augmentor, an accelerator programme for early-stage immersive technology companies, and through this programme helped another sixty companies move faster along their journeys to market. We appointed Mel Slater as a Catapult Fellow and we supported Imaginarium Studios to develop its leading-edge motion capture studio, which was founded and led by Andy Serkis (best known for playing Golam in *Lord of the Rings*).

Before our work on CreativeXR, Digital Catapult identified a second opportunity in VR and AR: the emerging art/science of performance capture. A new recording technique, volumetric capture, combined high-definition imagery with position and motion information, essentially allowing a performance to be captured in full video quality and then replayed within a virtual scene. It was evident that this could be crucial in making more compelling VR experiences. In 2017 there were only four companies in the world developing volumetric capture as a commercial proposition, and after researching each of them, it was clear that the market leader was Microsoft's Mixed Reality Capture Studio based in San Francisco.

So we teamed up with Microsoft and with Hammerhead VR, a small but innovative UK production company based in

Gateshead. Together we created Dimension, Europe's first production studio dedicated to volumetric performance capture. It was only the world's third such facility and the first to seek to take the technology commercial. There was no equivalent anywhere – not even in Los Angeles or New York – at the time. We were excited to be ahead of Hollywood.

Dimension made an immediate impact, attracting huge interest from a wide range of users. One early customer used it to make an AR training programme for nurses using Microsoft's HoloLens; others made VR episodes based on hit TV shows and still others made educational and music content. Our client list included Sky, NBC Universal, Pearson and the BBC, and soon Dimension Studio was known throughout the media and broadcast industries. Some of the first and most innovative applications came, surprisingly, from sports broadcasters. Sky, for example, used the technique to capture leading golfers' swings on the course – using a purpose-built mobile studio at the PGA Northern Ireland Open – to add a new element to the way that TV sports commentators were able to talk about the golfers' technique and skills.

Volumetric capture put Digital Catapult on the map too. Consumer VR was still in the doldrums, but suddenly people began to understand that we had created a facility from which an entire sector could benefit, helping to create a new generation of UK companies and bringing in deals and investment from all over the world. Our subsequent work with CreativeXR also led to more public investment being made in the form of a £30m project called Audience of the Future, under which the Arts and Humanities Research Council awarded substantial grants to six projects to create high-impact, location-based experiences, with the aim of achieving audiences of more than 150,000 for each.

But then came an unexpected blow to our plans, and everyone else's: the Covid-19 pandemic. In March 2020 every film and TV and VR production in the world was shut down. Once the initial shock of lockdown had worn off, many in the technology industry assumed that the flight to teleconferencing platforms, like Zoom, would be followed by a migration to still more immersive platforms. Given all that enforced locked-down time at home, you might have thought consumers would have jumped into VR, with its promise of flight from mundane reality. But price points were still high, content still thin and the experience still alienating at a time when people were craving more social interaction, not less, so there was little beyond an initial spike in headset sales.

However, the pandemic *did* stimulate an amazing growth of streaming video services. With consumers unable to get to cinemas or, for that matter, to any form of recreation beyond their front doors, there was an explosive increase in demand for screen-based entertainment. Netflix led the way, but soon every major tech company and Hollywood studio had its own streaming service: Amazon, Apple, Disney, HBO, Sky and so on. And that meant insatiable demand for the kind of ambitious high-end programming that would attract subscribers.

Making that programming would have been challenging at the best of times, but during a global pandemic it was almost impossible. Location shooting was fraught with expense and complexity – with even a single case of Covid requiring a shoot to come to a juddering halt, at eye-watering cost. Studio space was almost impossible to come by, the major production companies having already booked out space for years to come. So the industry was looking for any solution that might shorten production times, reduce budgets and ideally increase creative flexibility.

A few of the more technology savvy TV and film directors began to realise that they could use simulated environments to shoot pretty much any scene they liked from any angle they liked, and volumetric or motion capture to drop actors or digital assets into those environments. The missing piece was provided by game engines like Unity and Unreal made by Epic Games (the wealthy owner of *Fortnite*), software tools that are used to control the action and create the scenes they needed. By having actors perform in front of computer-controlled LED video screens, the game engines can calibrate shifting lighting and perspective. As characters perform in front of computer-generated scenery, the lights, camera positions and overall effects can be made to respond in a coordinated fashion. The result owed as much to animation as to live-action filmmaking; virtual production became an industry buzzword. Disney claimed the first full-length series to be produced using virtual production with its *Star Wars* spin-off, *The Mandalorian*.

The value of virtual production is that productions no longer need to send actors and full crew on location: you can shoot their scenes in the studio. If you want to shoot, say, a glorious sunset scene, you do not have to wait for the sunset and hope the clouds look right or that it doesn't start raining. Instead, you can shoot the sunset once, when conditions are right, and then have your actors perform in front of it as it is played out on an LED screen and controlled through a game engine. You can put the camera anywhere, to capture any facet of the actor's performance; and you can put the actor in any environment you can imagine (and render).

In short, you can save time and money, reduce carbon footprints and have more creative options than ever. This represents a radical disruption of media production – the kind of disruption envisaged under the Creative Industries Strategy we had begun to envisage ten years previously at the Technology Strategy Board (Chapter 7). And during the Covid pandemic, it proved invaluable in allowing production to continue with fewer crew on set and less location work. And the captured assets can be used in other contexts too – to make spin-off games or online interactive content.

But this intersection of the physical and digital went both ways. As well as putting real people into digital spaces, technology was also being developed to put digital features into the physical world. Augmented reality, like its virtual cousin, has a decades-long history – the first convincing AR system was built by the US Air Force in the early 1990s – and seized the public imagination with its depiction in futuristic films like 2002's *Minority Report*. But the general public didn't come face to face with it until the launch of Google Glass in 2014 – and they didn't like what they saw, or, more precisely, what Glass might see. Glass turned into a rare example of a Silicon Valley product that was roundly rejected as socially unacceptable, with users becoming the butt of hostile memes and real-world bans. Despite its futuristic appeal for some, many could not be persuaded that it was not creepily intrusive. Evidently the perpetual surveillance that we all ignore online is insufferable when it is literally in your face.

Meanwhile, buzz had been growing around the Florida-based start-up Magic Leap, which was said to be working on breakthrough AR technology using retinal display technology, which (crudely speaking) beams images directly into your eyes. In 2015, it released a succession of stunning demo videos, including one that showed a whale appearing out of nowhere and splashing down in the middle of an auditorium of awe-struck spectators. But the videos were only mock-ups and, despite attracting billions in investment from major players including Google – and staging staggeringly elaborate product launches, featuring cultural megastars including on one occasion *Snow Crash* author Neal Stephenson, with grandiose talk about the augmented planet and the 'magiverse' – when the underwhelming reality became clear three years later, the company went into a sharp decline and eventually lost 93% of its value.

So the Valley's usual techniques – shock and awe, hype and float – didn't work out. It was an intriguing indication that perhaps there is the potential for the next iteration of a digital existence to be created by newcomers or outsiders, using different playbooks to those that have propelled the past thirty years of growth.

Some of those other, less showy versions of AR have already started to make a mark, using the technology that is already at your fingertips. In 2016, swarms of people started mysteriously to congregate at seemingly random locations around the world. They were not truly random, of course: they were trying to 'catch 'em all' in *Pokémon Go*, the smartphone-based AR smash made by Niantic, a previously little-known US developer founded by ex-Google Maps executives and developers.

Lightning has yet to strike twice: no one has yet replicated Niantic's success with *Pokémon Go*, including Niantic itself. But AR is nonetheless creeping up on us. When you've just popped up from an underground station, the world can look quite disorienting. But if you open Google Maps on your phone, you can use an augmented reality overlay to show you which way to go, following arrows and labels overlaid on your view of the street, which you can only see via your screen. Such low-key applications – so low-key that no one even remarks on them as being augmented reality – may usher in the augmented age before anyone notices it is here.

In part, this is because they don't strike us as the lush graphics and sounds that we have been conditioned to expect, and that most developers strive for. The gradual creeping forward of higher and higher definition is something we've seen repeatedly in the development of TV, computer monitors and phone screens, and in the increasingly faithful quality of audio. But it's not actually necessary. We have already seen that the quality of rendering and the degree of verisimilitude does not necessarily deter audiences from engaging. Mp3 audio is of poor sound quality compared with a CD but that didn't stop it ruling the world. *Minecraft* and *Fortnite* are crude and pixelated, but no one cares: in fact, it's part of their charm.

That won't be true in all areas, of course. In some areas realism is not just desirable but mandatory: telesurgery, for example. So we will see progress being made unevenly, precisely because there is such a wide and diverse set of applications for these technologies. Eventually we might be able to access environments and objects that are all but indistinguishable from reality, anywhere and anytime. But our introductions to virtual media are likely to be through more unassuming spaces.

As with the software, so with hardware. High-end gear like Google Glass and HoloLens struggled to secure mass adoption. Magic Leap was all but dead on arrival, and Apple has yet to enter the market despite endless rumours and the bundling of its ARKit with all iPhones. But cheaper, lower spec eyewear is on its way, with less ambitious goals: those made by Nreal, for example, prioritise streaming media over virtual or augmented reality. In due course, these may provide a 'stealth' introduction to augmented reality, and perhaps to the virtual worlds beyond. And so we wait for the hardware and the physics to catch up as we stand at the doors of the metaverse.

Twins and things

{'Heaven or Las Vegas', Cocteau Twins,
Heaven or Las Vegas, 1990}

Real actors playing fictional people becoming digital humans within simulated worlds standing in for real locations. The line between the real and the virtual is becoming more blurred. Already we have Instagram influencers like Lil Miquela, who leads a lively online life while pitching fashion brands to her legions of followers. It doesn't take too much effort to work out that Miquela is computer-generated, but everyone seems happy to play along. Meanwhile, rumours persist that other computer-generated hypebeasts have yet to be detected, although that claim may itself be hype. Is this blurring of the line between reality and simulation a good idea?

In 2017, I had a most unsettling experience courtesy of Mel Slater, one of the first and most thoughtful researchers of virtual reality and the effect on its users. I went to Barcelona to visit Slater in his lab where he had been working with the Department of Justice of Catalonia. He described one of his experiments to me and offered me a go. Having donned the VR headset, I found myself standing in the entrance hall of a house, unsure of what to expect – until a man came in the front door as if arriving home from work. Immediately on seeing me, he began to shout and gesture aggressively, looming ever closer over my virtual self – although I felt very much as though it was my actual self who was being threatened, not my digital double. Attempting to speak or look away drew further abuse and eventually he came right up into my face. It really felt like an invasion of my personal space – I shied away. It was with some relief that after twenty minutes I was able to remove the headset and re-enter the real world.

This simulation was designed not for the general public, but for people – inevitably, men – who had been convicted of domestic abuse. By putting them in the position of their victims, Slater showed how he could show the offenders the experience of their victims. Before the experience, offenders were markedly less likely to recognise fear in their victims' faces; afterwards, they were much more likely to understand it. The follow-up evidence was even more striking: of the control group who were not exposed to his programme but only attended the obligatory series of lectures, the majority showed no change in behaviour. The group who had the VR experience displayed an 80% reduction in recidivism. Over a period of three years Slater worked with more than 300 offenders to demonstrate the impact of this approach. His research continues longitudinally to ascertain how lasting the effects will be.

Slater and other researchers have since demonstrated, using proven neuroscientific devices in VR, that VR body transference can be made to occur very quickly so that the person in the VR experience physically identifies with an avatar, which may be of another gender or race or even species. Simulations have been used to encourage generosity towards the homeless, to reduce the effects of implicit bias in jury trials and to help understand the effects of paranoid delusions. Slater has even created simulations that enable you to talk to yourself, face-to-face, as a therapeutic tool. This research and its powerful effectiveness have led some to refer to VR as an 'empathy engine'. In fact the phrase was probably coined by Jeremy Bailenson, the founder of the Virtual Human Interaction Lab at Stanford University. I first met Bailenson in late 2017 when I visited his lab to learn about his research and the many companies he is helping to develop commercial VR applications.

VR is gradually establishing itself as a regular tool in

industry for a variety of tasks, but in particular for training. It has moved well beyond research and is now widely used to train personnel in the military, for hazardous industrial environments and in retail. Bailenson was closely involved in the development of a training programme for Walmart staff. The retailer was faced with the tricky problem of training its staff to deal with large-scale customer incursions such as tend to take place when there are special promotions, such as on Black Friday. Using VR, Bailenson was able to help the company create realistic scenarios in VR in which the customer service or sales staff needed to intervene. The project was piloted in one store and proved so successful that it was rolled out to all Walmart facilities across the United States.

Clearly, these examples demonstrate how the outputs of academic research can be applied to positive effect.

Following Slater's research into the ability of VR to have a positive impact on cognitive behaviour, a group of us met with him to discuss the further implications of enhancing empathy through body transference in the kind of ultra-realistic environment enabled by volumetric capture and anticipated in some of the visions of the metaverse. Our discussion raised interesting questions about the degree of impact that these kinds of narratives might have in more realistic environments. We asked whether the impact might be longer lasting as a result.[1]

As yet, we have no collective answers to these questions. Bailenson's concerns about the power of VR to alter mental states are such that he advises people against spending more than twenty minutes at a time inside virtual worlds. This is in complete contradiction to the metaverse maximalists who believe we should spend our entire waking, or at least working, lives immersed in a virtual world. Clearly, the concern must also be that if VR experiences can be created with the intention of positively altering cognitive behaviour, the opposite could also be induced.

For obvious reasons, no one has experimented with making abusers *worse*, dehumanising the homeless or heightening mental illness. And yet what we have learned from the past two decades is that if there is a dark side to be exploited, it will be. Consider that a social network initially intended to let people chat with family and friends ended up fomenting an insurrection in the world's most powerful democracy. VR may be an empathy engine, but perhaps it can also be used as a dehumanisation engine.

We already have evidence that the technology may be used to negative effects. 'Deepfakes' is the popular name for AI-powered simulations that make real people appear to say and do things they never said or did. This has many useful applications – in humanising otherwise unfriendly online interactions by generating virtual customer service assistants, for example, or allowing one person to 'speak' in many different languages. But deepfakes can also be used to simulate degrading actions. Once again it is women and minority groups who are the victims.

It does not matter if the deepfakes are not particularly convincing: the aim is to turn them into an object at the perpetrator's mercy – to dehumanise. This is dangerous even if the victim never sees it, or even if *no one* ever sees it but its creator. Dehumanisation is often cited as a factor in hate speech online, where people are reduced to words on a screen; it is certainly a factor in real-world atrocities like sexual violence and ethnic cleansing. It might seem a stretch to connect the two, but once again, remember: Facebook used to be a place where you went to throw imaginary sheep at your friends. Now it is where conspiracy theorists and extremists congregate.

So although no one wants to cramp the potential of

immersive technology, we need to think very carefully about how it will be used. There's still incredible ignorance and naivety about the impact of this kind of experience: my usual optimism that it will just work out fine as it becomes an every-day consumer technology is perhaps misplaced.

We should not forget that there are plenty of powerful applications for the technology – and not just for entertainment. A metaverse will not only be a place to tell stories, hang out or play games: it might also contain houses and factories or remote diagnosis and mental health services. It also has industrial applications, where the language changes but the underlying enabling technologies and the skills needed to operate them are the same. In industry, different sectors are actively exploring ways to solve problems and make savings through the creation of digital twins. Expanding on traditional ideas of data mod-elling and computer simulation, the idea of digital twins is to use much higher levels of data granularity to reproduce real objects (a jet engine) or complex environments (a city) to speed up prototyping, solve design or planning problems, or predict maintenance issues.

Thanks to the scanning and simulation technologies we have developed over the past decade, we can now create a facility that could model and simulate every aspect of a physical item (e.g. a jet engine) before it is created. We might also be able to synthe-sise all the environmental factors it might have to negotiate (the weather conditions a plane might have to fly in); we can visual-ise all the possible interactions with this item (the birds it might fly into, different landing and take-off conditions). And we can then optimise it to manage all those factors as completely as possible – all before we create even one physical prototype. This is the ultimate dream of every designer, every architect and every engineer. But as I talked to colleagues in Silicon Valley and asked them who is really leading in this field, it seems that very few companies are yet convincing leaders in this space.

The canonical use for this kind of application is in aviation. Aircraft are made up of incredibly complex and expensive parts that have to perform flawlessly. Designing, making and testing them is rightly a long and rigorous process. Being able to create a simulated part and seeing how it performs in simulations can cut out a lot of trial and error before a prototype is ready to go into a wind tunnel. Conversely, we can embed an existing part – an engine, say – to monitor its condition in real time, remotely, running its digital twin to see how it performs. And we can use the digital twin as a model to allow engineers to inspect it and service it more thoroughly and efficiently, using augmented reality headsets to make sure they follow the steps needed for checks, repairs and fault detection.

Virtualisation can be used in the automotive sector, urban planning, aerospace and machine engineering as well as in film, television, advertising and games. In some respects, the only difference will be whether the finished product is a digital product or a physical one. But all the design and engineering that might go into making the product could be similar and use similar technologies. The real question yet to be worked through here, though, is: how much data do you need to make the twin effective? If you have to replicate reality 1:1, then there would be unlikely to be much of a saving.

This is both exciting and highly challenging in relation to the supply of skilled and trained technicians capable of providing this kind of service. It requires the emergence of a whole new sector of companies, tools and products, with a proven business model that understands the level of digital twinning that has to be achieved in order to provide value, without costing the planet.

For better or for worse, we will soon be able to put real and/ or digital people into real and/or digital environments, filled with real and/or digital objects. How much we wish to participate in this remains to be seen, as does the exact means of our participation. But the distinction between the digital and physical worlds will have been eroded considerably if not become irrelevant. We will soon be neighbouring the metaverse.

That seems to be the assumption among the technology giants, anyway. Mark Zuckerberg is so convinced that the metaverse is the future that he rebranded his entire company to 'Meta'. Microsoft's ownership of LinkedIn, *Minecraft* and the HoloLens platform suggests virtual aspirations, while Google and Apple are assumed to be quietly tooling up too. Entertainment companies are getting in on the action: Epic Games, maker of *Fortnite* and the enabling technology platform Unreal Engine, has taken investment from Sony. Hardware manufacturers including HTC Vive and Nvidia are developing devices, tools and platforms too.

All these companies are betting big that the metaverse or a series of metaverses will constitute Web 3.0 or vice versa as technological and creative research and development continue, and as the kinds of immersive experiments pioneered under programmes like CreativeXR make their way into the mainstream. But the other massive driver of the advent of metaverse environments is the huge influx of investment in cryptocurrencies and non-fungible tokens that is accompanying the technology convergence we've been exploring. Given the collective clout of some of the major corporations already making waves in this space and the flood of investment, the advent of metaverse-like environments is likely to be a self-fulfilling prophecy. The question for the rest of us is: what kind of metaverse or metaverses do we want?

Making the metaverse

{'Heaven', Talking Heads, *Fear of Music*, 1979}

The concept of the metaverse foresees the same kind of potential to shift paradigms that the world wide web had. The vision of the metaverse maximalists is a parallel, synthetic environment in which an entire universe can be rendered in real time with no lag, no proxies, no substitutions. This is the ultimate extension of the internet and of virtual reality worlds, populated not by avatars or animations, but by characters, animals and physical items rendered with absolute verisimilitude – interactive digital humans who are impossible to differentiate from the real thing. It is the ultimate and perfect product of a god-like impulse to create and control. It is a combination of the kinds of vision foreseen in science fiction films like *Blade Runner* and *The Matrix*.

That the metaverse's sights and sounds will be more real than real is a given; but it could also be enhanced by scents created through olfactory devices and replete with powerful touch sensors and haptics to create the sensation of a breeze brushing your hair or the deep rumble of thunder. But who will create, and who will control, these metaverses of the future?

One answer comes at the level of geopolitics. I sometimes refer to what we're building as the Great Western Metaverse. That's partly as a nod to the scale of the engineering challenge, which reminds me of the Great Western Railway, built by Isambard Kingdom Brunel. There are many technical challenges to be overcome before the above vision of the metaverse becomes possible. But given enough time, ingenuity and money – all three of which are for the moment in plentiful supply – they will be.

But it's also out of respectful acknowledgement that China

and its allies are busily constructing an equally powerful and differently oriented metaverse of their own. Barring a sudden change of policy, that metaverse will likely be much more designed to increase state control first, and facilitate culture and industry second. China, after all, already uses surveillance technologies like deep-packet inspection and facial recognition to monitor its people to a degree that no Western government has yet countenanced. Having proven implacable in enforcing lockdowns and suppressing its Uighur population, it is hard to see why the Chinese government would relax its grip now.

Those of us in the West have our own decisions to make. The world wide web was free and open before it was walled up, the cyberpunk fantasy of endless possibility giving way to digital medievalism. The choice before us is whether we permit the metaverse to be the continuation of this process, or if we attempt to reverse the trend and decide collectively that we really want an open, interoperable metaverse inside which these others could coexist. If we do, then we have to support those who are actively looking to build that version of the metaverse. The choice is still there to be made, because the metaverse does not exist yet.

The internet began as a defence industry experiment, became an academic tool and then burst into the public sphere when Tim Berners-Lee decided to create a more user-friendly way to navigate it. Its history is largely one of accident and happenstance. The metaverse, by contrast, is being conceived upfront. No one knows exactly how it will turn out, but we don't have to wait and see: we can decide.

And we have seen that although Big Tech may have the power and the money, and to some extent the expertise and talent, it does not have any automatic guarantee of success. Facebook's transformation into Meta has not been popular, attracting derision for its tedious and occasionally tone-deaf demonstrations. Google's Glass was so offputting that its users became known as 'glassholes' and were barred from certain bars and restaurants. Conversely, the biggest successes in virtual reality and augmented reality have come from games producers like Epic and Niantic, running on comparatively generic hardware. Content may yet prove to be king.

Even if Big Tech does win the day, we will most likely have not one metaverse, but several. Each of the titans, and most likely a few newcomers, will make its own virtual world. There will be precious little interoperability: data will be unlikely to be able to move freely from one world to another, just as data cannot move freely between social media platforms today. You will be able to create and trade within the walls of a particular world, but it is unlikely that you will be able to trade beyond them. You will be incentivised, by fair means or foul, to spend as long as possible in its VR or AR environments. Like the Hotel California in the Eagles' song, you'll be able to check in any time you like but never leave, whatever the cognitive effects on your psyche.

Or it might be that we choose a more open model. Some of the leaders in immersive technology and content – including Niantec, Epic and Roblox – have been discussing models where the metaverse is a marketplace, in which a set of agreed technical standards creates a shared space for individual experiences while allowing smaller businesses to sell products and services. This would not be so different from the way that in-game economies work already, but the transactions might be for more serious purposes than powering up an avatar, or creating a custom home to hang out in. Virtual rent, user subscriptions and third-party advertising could support the running costs of the shared space.

But we could go further still – all the way back to the cyber-punk vision of a fully open and entirely interoperable metaverse. Back in the early noughties, when it was becoming apparent that the media was going to be irreversibly disrupted by the arrival of the internet, there were discussions about creating what was variously called a national publisher or a national-ised web platform. There was precedent for this not only in the form of state broadcasters, but with early data services like the UK's Teletext and France's Minitel. As the control exerted by the GAFA companies over the internet itself became more obvious, people at the BBC – the world's pre-eminent public service media organisation – started to muse about the pos-sibility of 'a public digital space'.

In the event, we got neither a national web platform nor a public digital space. The free market seemed to be thriving, with the Valley ecosystem, driven by venture capital, throwing up technological miracles and business success stories faster than anyone could keep track of them. There seemed to be ample opportunity for companies to experiment, and thus little need to direct taxpayers' money into a ring-fenced environment in which public good might be more of a driver than private gain. Later it became apparent that network effects meant most start-ups would either never be able to compete with the existing powerhouses, or would have to blitz-scale their way to impressive fortunes built on shaky foundations. But by then it was too late.

Now we are entering a similarly exciting, and challenging, period. Technology that could transform how we live and work is on the horizon. Its front-runners have already captured the public imagination, in the form of cryptocurrencies and NFTs, or immersive worlds like *Fortnite* and *Roblox* – even if they are not necessarily particularly practical introductions to the technology. But this time we are coming to it with much greater awareness that new technology has costs as well as benefits, and arguably much greater inclination to think twice before we jump into the metaverse.

And that's why I remain excited, in a naively idealistic way, that we are about to see an explosion of opportunities not just in the realms of media and entertainment, but across the industrial landscape in all sorts of different applications. We can make the metaverse what we want it to be.

To avoid the mistakes of the past, we will have to push to make the metaverse a truly open environment, not multiple, mutually incompatible worlds that lock us in, where everything from the digital clothes on our backs to the virtual objects we trade are not ultimately owned and controlled by one giant corporation or another. The right to be disconnected, to go offline, may become as prized as the right to be connected was a decade ago. Even as we push for an open metaverse, we also will need to pursue the right not to be tracked, not to have to give up personal information to access the simplest of services.

David Chalmers in his 2022 book, *Reality+: Virtual Worlds and the Problems of Philosophy* (Norton and Co, Jan 2022), makes the argument that virtual reality and reality are essentially the same, that our behaviours in one are mirrors of our behaviours in the other and therefore require the same kind of social governance and that we can therefore live meaningful lives in VR. While I enjoy the philosophical convolutions that Chalmers explores, he ignores the fundamentals of the impact of business models on virtual environments. The question of whether our whole 'natural' experience is just a simulation of someone else's making is certainly fun to play with. Douglas Adams in *Hitchhiker's Guide to the Galaxy* suggested that the human condition is probably just a vast experiment being conducted by extra-terrestrial white mice.

As we have seen throughout this book, the importance of the values conferred on a business by its business model cannot be underestimated. There is a naivety in David Chalmers' position which seems to ignore the behavioural influence that Meta's advertising revenue model brings to bear on all its users. If interests and favourites being tracked inside Facebook make for unsavoury targeted ads and content streaming, the world of Oculus in which every participant's physical biometrics are tracked and interpreted to serve the interests of the business model is even more alarming. It's no longer a question of whether we can live meaningful lives or not in virtual reality, it's whether we are wide open to manipulation and influence by a fully immersive environment.

A public interest metaverse that could support public services and spaces for both cultural expression and industrial experiment may seem utopian and idealistic. But if we don't push in that direction now, we will waste an opportunity to maximise the benefit of not just one, but several digital technologies as expansive as the internet, but with potentially even greater powers of social transformation and economic rebalancing. An universally accessible market; a level playing field with permanently lowered barriers to entry, where data sharing will be *de rigueur*: an open, public metaverse could be a place where values-driven businesses are better able to thrive, where a more inclusive and diverse workforce can come together with fewer prejudices or preconceptions about the way things should be done and more awareness of how amazing it could be 'if we did it this way'.

As we reach the end of this book, I have had to pause a couple of times and ask myself if I'm not being disingenuous, or naïve, in making these arguments. I have had to ask myself if everyone really just wants to make loads of money and that arguing for more is some kind of refusal to acknowledge that. Some may indeed think that way and they're free to do so, but I really do believe that the shock of the pandemic, the rise of social justice movements like #MeToo and #BlackLivesMatter, the LGBTQ+ movement, and the worsening climate emergency have had an enormous impact on how we think about our careers, and indeed our lives. And whilst I don't think that they should lead inevitably to a Great Resignation, what they are doing is to engender a radical rethink of what we need to do in our work and in our lives.

These themes, in powerful combination, have led to a deep shift in consciousness not just around working practices but also in how we treat each other and why we are in business at all. Covid may have given us the shove we needed to shed our addiction to the internet, or it may have pushed us into ever more immersion in the digital world. Either way, we cannot go back to the way things were. Our social, political and economic divisions, and the fallacy of trying to heal these by leaving business to the most aggressive and least conscientious, are starker than they have ever been. The inevitability of progress is not a given. In our lifetimes we have seen reductions in technological capability (like supersonic transatlantic flights for example) and reductions in human rights (such as the appalling decision by the US Supreme Court to overturn Roe v Wade) in our most apparently progressive societies.

But we have to remain optimistic and believe that if we can find the ways to navigate successfully through our present predicament and if we stay thoughtful and intuitive about the lessons the pandemic years have taught us, as well as those we have learned from thirty years of breakneck technological and commercial development, we could perhaps remake the world for ourselves in a better form. We could see an extraordinary flowering of new forms of creativity, new industrial ambition and capability, newly reinvigorated and equitable workplaces, new ways to socialise, mobilise and respect each other's differences, to trade and play and live our hybrid digital and physical lives. In short, we could realise the full richness and unlimited potential of a values-based digital culture. That would be a digital rebirth: a digital renaissance.

D-REN PLAYLIST

open.spotify.com/playlist/7zz4d4ZtaY9XSJ
MFkeQm1U?si=a3418d324b864d8d

Introduction
'For What It's Worth', Buffalo Springfield, 1966

Into cyberspace
'Starman', David Bowie, *The Rise and Fall of Ziggy Stardust and the Spiders from Mars*, 1972

Jacking in
'I've Seen That Face Before (Libertango)', Grace Jones, *Nightclubbing*, 1981

Working for the man
'Jarabi', Ketama and Toumani Diabate, *Songhai*, 1988

The Raft
'Papua New Guinea', The Future Sound of London, *Accelerator*, 1991

Ahead of the curve
'My Squelchy Life', Brian Eno, *Nerve Net*, 1992

Dotcom revolution
'Teardrop', Massive Attack, *Mezzanine*, 1998

Time to take my shot
'Wake Up', Rage Against the Machine, 1992

A brush with the law
'Watching the Detectives', Elvis Costello, *My Aim is True*,
    1977

You wouldn't steal a car
'Nagoya Marimbas', Steve Reich, *Striking a Balance*, 1998

The trojan horse
'Yamore', Salif Keita and Cesaria Evora, *Mofou*, 2002

Creative communities
Variations on a Theme of Frank Bridge, Benjamin Britten and
    the English Chamber Orchestra, 1969

Stepping up to the plate
'Blue Train', John Coltrane, *Blue Train*, 1958

From Finsbury Park to the world
'Games People Play', King Curtis, Instant Groove, 1969

Exit, pursued by a bear
'Crazy', Gnarls Barkley, *St Elsewhere*, 2006

Cardboard to cloud
'Muy Tranquilo', Gramatik, *SB3*, 2010

Power to the people
'This Is the 21st Century', Marillion, *Anoraknophobia*, 2001

Back to reality
'15 Step', Radiohead, *In Rainbows*, 2007

We all stand together?
'Echoes', Pink Floyd, *Meddle*, 1971

Herding creative cats
'Smile', Lily Allen, *Alright, Still*, 2006

The wisdom of crowds
'Do It With a Rockstar', Amanda Palmer and the Grand Theft
    Orchestra, *Theatre Is Evil*, 2012

Emotional corporations
'Babel', Mumford & Sons, *Babel*, 2012

Do it yourself
'Half Life', Imogen Heap, *Ellipse*, 2009

Intuition and investment
'Mr Jones', Talking Heads, *Naked*, 1988

On death and dying
'Gimme Shelter', The Rolling Stones, *Let It Bleed*, 1969

Tarzan economics
'Empire State of Mind (Part II) Broken Down', Alicia Keyes,
    The Element of Freedom, 2009

By the numbers
'Anaconda', Nicki Minaj, *The Pinkprint*, 2014

Supply and demand
'Pirate Bay', Netsky, 2010

Data, data, data
'Happy', Pharrell Williams, *Girl*, 2014

Selling up
'Uptown Funk', Mark Ronson, *Uptown Special*, 2015

Digital medieval
'Rio Grande', Ikebe Shakedown, *Stone by Stone*, 2014

Reinventing innovation
'Christopher Walken on Sunshine', Shawn Lee, Princess
    Superstar, *Sing a Song*, 2010

Going public
'Get Free', The Clubcasa Chamber Orchestra, Sly5thAve, 2015

What governments want
'Cody', Mogwai, *Government Commissions – BBC Sessions,*
    1996–2003, 2005

Reloading the catapult
'Into the Dark', Marc Moulin, *Top Secret*, 2001

The innovation landscape
'Gnossienne', Paolo Fresu, Richard Galliano, Jan Lundgren,
    Mare Nostrum II, 2016

Business unusual
'Kokoro', Fatoumata Diawara, *Fenfo (Something to Say)*,
    2018

Growing pains
'Adhara', Mop Mop, *Lunar Love*, 2016

Mousetraps and models
'Mambo Sinuendo', Ry Cooder, Manuel Galban, *Mambo
    Sinuendo*, 2003

Platform power
'Alegntaye', Akale Wube, *Sost*, 2014

Do the right thing
'Ballad of a Thin Man', Bob Dylan, *Live at Budokan*, 1979

Culture clash
'Clint Eastwood', Ed Case / Sweetie Irie refix, *Gorillaz*, 2001

Squeezed out
'Cler Achel', Tinariwen, *Aman Iman*, 2006

Creative block
'Angelo', Shai Maestro, *Shai Maestro Trio*, 2013

Beyond reach
'Cool Struttin'', Sonny Collins, *Cool Struttin'*, 1958

Return to core values
'Yillah', Hadouk Trio with Steve Shehan, *Air Hadouk*, 2010

Back to reality
'The Silent Flight of the Owl', Manu Delago, *Circadian*, 2019

Building worlds
'Aisatsana', Aphex Twin, *Syro*, 2014

Virtually there
'Virtual World', Verve, *A Storm in Heaven*, 1993

Twins and things
'Heaven or Las Vegas', Cocteau Twins, *Heaven or Las Vegas*, 1990

Making the metaverse
'Heaven', Talking Heads, *Fear of Music*, 1979

NOTES

1. Into cyberspace

1. That was somewhat true. Hacker culture began with 'phone phreaking', finding ways to do things that weren't supposed to be done with telephones – particularly making free long-distance calls from public phone boxes. Until recently *2600*, the hacker magazine, still featured celebratory photographs of obscure-looking phone boxes from exotic locations on its back cover.

2. This dynamic was to repeat in the mp3 era. Because digital files cost little or nothing to make and distribute, the prices being asked for them by record companies seemed extortionate, and so many people saw little wrong with turning to free, if often unauthorised, alternatives.

3. Sanders, one of the UK's pioneers in internet music, went on to establish a label called the state51 Conspiracy, as well as Consolidated Independent, which today is one of Europe's leading digital distribution platforms.

4. Curry is now one of the UK's leading futurists.

2. Dotcom revolution

1. In 2007, AT&T ended up negotiating to be the exclusive US distributor of Apple's revolutionary iPhone across the United States. If AT&T had paid closer attention to Larry Miller a

decade earlier, it might have been AT&T licensing the iPhone to Apple Computer, rather than the other way around. Miller is now Professor of Music Management at NYU.

2. The BitTorrent file-sharing technology that enabled Napster was also used in the early version of the Spotify platform to help reduce network costs.

3. Algorithmic curation went on to rule the world – something one of my later companies, Semetric, was to play a part in (see Chapter 6) – but at the time it would have been laughably bad. So Uplister was powered by people.

4. See, for example, Stephen Witt's book *How Music Got Free: The Inventor, the Mogul, and the Thief* (Vintage, 2016).

5. Payola (undeclared, and illegal, payments to DJs to play certain songs) is the best-known example of this influence, but the industry had a host of other perfectly legal but ethically whiffy ways to direct broadcasters.

4. Power to the people

1. Songwriters and composers stood to benefit from this new diffuse economic environment, albeit at a greater remove.

2. The idea of internet access as a fundamental right raised eyebrows in 2009, but today an increasing number of essential government services have moved online-only, so it proved not to have been a stretch after all.

3. The slow burn that makes crowdfunded projects appealing to fans is ill suited to impulse purchasing or instant gratification. Buying on the basis of a pitch and waiting months for the product to arrive is a world away from hearing something on the radio and buying it that afternoon or downloading it thirty seconds later.

4. One unexpected by-product was the emerging obviousness

of bands formed by middle-class kids, in contrast to the traditional mythology of talent emerging from street corners, housing estates and tenements.

5. Emotional corporations

1. *System Error: Where Big Tech Went Wrong and How We Can Reboot*, R. Reich, M. Sahami and J.M. Weinstein (Harper, 2021).

6. By the numbers

1. The next killer app for social platforms was the combination of smartphone cameras and mobile broadband. This time, Facebook didn't hang about: Facebook bought Instagram before it could become a real competitive threat.
2. These difficulties were not unique to music. Most notoriously, Tumblr (for blogging) and Flickr (for photos), both much loved by their many users, completely lost their way after being acquired by Yahoo! and never recovered.

10. Back to reality

1. 'The ethics of realism in virtual and augmented reality', M. Slater et al., *Frontiers in Virtual Reality*, March 2020.

ACKNOWLEDGEMENTS

This book is an attempt to make some sense of a series of experiences that I happened to have had over a few decades in the world of music, technology and innovation, combined with an analysis of what it might take to be a successful entrepreneur, which forms of success might turn out to be more sustainable, and how the varied agendas of founders, investors, politicians and industrialists diverge and converge in different ways at different times.

All of this is seen through the rapidly changing lenses of ever evolving technologies which inevitably enter the world disruptively and make unpredictable impacts on business models and business methodologies. As the madness of metaverse mania threatens to overwhelm us all, I have tried to extrapolate forward and suggest what responsible business and responsible use of metaverse technologies might look like and what we might try to avoid in the future context of the metaverse and web 3.0.

There are a lot of people to thank whose help and support I'd like to acknowledge here. Sumit Paul-Choudhury worked tirelessly with me on preparing much of this book. He interviewed me and transcribed, then edited and ordered my words, made my ramblings more rational and sifted key arguments from varied opinions, while I tried to hold down my dayjob at the Catapult. I am incredibly grateful to him for putting so much into this and helping me present these thoughts and analyses more cogently and at times with more back-up evidence than I could manage on my own. Amanda Kamin, Chief of Marcoms at Digital Catapult and Peter Jones of Profile Books helped the book into the form you now see it in, and it would be a weaker book without them both. I'd like to thank all the artists, managers and other friends and associates in the music industry who influenced my thinking and put up with my ramblings, in particular, Tim Clerk, Peter Jenner, and Brian Message who each have done so much to change industry attitudes over the years. Thank you to the indefatigable Paul Pacifico for his boundless energy and enthusiasm for trying to make the world of the artist and creator a better place. Thanks to Paul Sanders, Boyd Steemson, Simon Hopkins and Matthew Brown for the endless banter and willingness to philosophise and wax lyrical on almost every topic discussed in these pages and many more. Thanks to all my colleagues at Digital Catapult, especially the Senior Leadership team, incredible people in an extraordinary institution, which has a life of its own – distinctive, unique, eclectic and passionate about its mission.

And of course, last but not least, thanks and hugs to my wife, Sue, whose love and encouragement pushed me to keep going when the end, at times, did not seem to be anywhere in sight! And of course, my kids Otto and Cora, who continue to be an inspiration.

There are many sources acknowledged and unconsciously drawn from here, but if there are errors in the book then they are, of course, all entirely mine.

OMISSIONS

There are also many things which I don't talk about at all in the book, which I should just mention here. I once introduced Brian Eno to Tony Blair, I lost Meat Loaf in a limestone cave near Beaconsfield, I introduced a little-known drag artist called RuPaul to the UK's media by having him throw croissants from the staircase of the Hotel Martinez in Cannes, I stood by David Bowie as he went into a booth in a Mayfair art gallery to sign a new contract with EMI Records, I watched from the wings as Jarvis Cocker climbed up Michael Jackson's stage set during his live performance at the Brit Awards, I was back stage when the band, the KLF, machine-gunned the audience at the BRITS with blanks and threw buckets of sheep's blood at them, I met Eduardo Paolozzi in the building site of the British Library when he came to present the maquette of his statue of Blake's *Newton*, I spent an hour and a half talking to film director, David Fincher about virtual production to help screenwriter and Peaky Blinders creator, Steven Knight sell him a film project in Birmingham. I was allowed to shake hands with Janet Jackson at the Roof Gardens nightclub in London, I had dinner with Bryan Ferry at La Mamounia Hotel in Marrakech, I almost abandoned a photoshoot with Anton Corbijn when Steve Winwood refused to come out of a caravan in New Orleans. I once took the Spice Girls to a Lenny Kravitz show at the Brixton Academy. Mentioning these things, serves almost no purpose – except I thought you'd just like to know – all in an innovator's day's work.

Jeremy Silver, *August 2022*

INDEX